I0455915

PATHWAY TO THE PODIUM

How to Win a U.S. Election

by
Howie Todoit

Copyright 2023 Archieboy Holdings, LLC. All rights reserved.

No part of this book may be reproduced in any form or by any electronic or mechanical means including information storage and retrieval systems, without permission in writing from the author. The only exception is by a reviewer, who may quote short excerpts in a review.

Although the author and publisher have made every effort to ensure that the information in this book was correct at press time, the author and publisher do not assume and hereby disclaim any liability to any party for any loss, damage, or disruption caused by errors or omissions, whether such errors or omissions result from negligence, accident, or any other cause.

This publication is designed to provide accurate and authoritative information with regard to the subject matter covered. It is sold with the understanding that the publisher is not engaged in rendering professional services. If legal advice or other expert assistance is required, the services of a competent professional should be sought.

The fact that an organization or website is referred to in this work as a citation and/or a potential source of further information does not mean that the author or the publisher endorses the information the organization or website may provide or recommendations it may make.

Please remember that Internet websites listed in this work may have changed or disappeared between when this work was written and when it is read.

Dear Esteemed Reader,

Thank you immensely for choosing this book to join your collection. We imagine that you've already embarked on an exploration of ideas within these pages, and we couldn't be happier about it!

Now, if you find yourself chuckling, pondering, or even debating with the words in front of you, we'd absolutely love to hear about it. If you can spare a few moments to pen down your thoughts in a review, we would be as delighted as a dictionary on a spelling bee!

An Amazon review would be excellent - but hey, we're far from picky. Whether it's a scribble on the back of a grocery list, a tweet, or even a message in a bottle (though that might take a while to reach us), your feedback is gold.

Writing a review might not be as fun as a spontaneous dance-off, but we promise it'll bring grins to our faces, warmth to our hearts, and incredibly valuable insights to future readers.

With Gratitude,

Bo Bennett, PhD
Publisher
Archieboy Holdings, LLC.

Table of Contents

Introduction

Welcome to the first step of your journey in developing your political career. Our goal with this book is to give you a comprehensive understanding of how to run for office in the United States and win. With a democratic political system rooted in representation, running for office is not merely about power; it's about trying to make a difference, about giving voice to the voiceless, and about participating in a governing system that has influenced the world over.

We're not going to sugar-coat it – running for office is not easy. It requires dedication, passion, a deep understanding of issues, and a commitment to serve the people. It's a challenging sprint towards an honorable and rewarding goal, and we're here to guide you every step of the way.

The guide is set up to move you progressively through the stages of launching a political career. Whether you are aspiring to become the next county commissioner, state governor, member of Congress, or even the President, this guide will provide you the key insights needed to build and run a successful campaign.

First off, we offer a primer on the United States political system in Chapter 1. It's essential to understand the architecture of this system and how the different levels of government interact. The role of political parties also can't be overstated, as they often can provide support and resources to aspiring politicians.

In Chapter 2, we dive into the different types of elections – from the presidential bout to the races of Senate, House of Representatives,

State, and Local Elections. Each type of election has its intricacies, and understanding these can give you a competitive edge.

Deciding your political career direction is covered in Chapter 3. Here, we advise on self-analysis techniques to identify your strengths and assist in choosing the right office that suits your leadership skills and values.

No political campaign can succeed without a dedicated and skilled team. In Chapter 4, we discuss the roles of the campaign manager, policy advisors, and media and public relations professionals – each making unique contributions toward your success.

Developing a political platform that resonates with voters is arguably one of the most demanding aspects of running for office. In Chapter 5, we break down how to understand mainstream issues and represent voter interests to earn their trust and votes.

Following that, Chapter 6 demystifies campaign fundraising, an intimidating but crucial aspect of your campaign. Understanding campaign finance laws will keep you on the right side of the law, while identifying donors and holding fundraisers will keep the campaign wheels turning.

Building voter support is the lifeblood of any campaign, and Chapter 7 provides effective voter outreach strategies, detailing how grassroots mobilization and social media can be harnessed for your advantage.

Then we pivot to helping you master public speaking in Chapter 8, so you can craft impactful speeches and handle media interviews with confidence and charisma.

Political debates can make or break a campaign, and in Chapter 9, you will find guidance on preparing for debates and adopting successful debating strategies.

Chapter 10 calls attention to the 'home stretch' - the closing moments leading to election day, including a look at final campaign pushes and election day logistics.

Post-election analysis is as crucial as any part of the campaign process. In Chapter 11, we provide insights on learning from election results and planning for the future, whether it ended in a win or a loss.

Finally, Chapter 12 serves as a trove of additional tips to help you triumph in U.S. elections.

By the end of this journey, our hope is that you'll be informed, empowered, and ready to venture out into the course of running for public office in the United States. And always remember: this is a path of service above all. Best of luck!

Chapter 1:
Understanding the
U.S. Political System

Heading straight into the heart of American politics, we first need a firm grasp on the basics of the U.S. political system. A labyrinthine world in itself, it's divided primarily into three branches—the Executive, the Legislative, and the Judicial, each wielding powers carefully measured to prevent dominance. The President, the head of the Executive branch, steers the country's affairs, but not without checks and balances from our Legislative branch (Congress with its Senate and House of Representatives) and our Judicial branch (led by the Supreme Court). Diving one layer deeper, you find two elephants in the room—or rather, a Donkey and Elephant, representing our Democratic and Republican parties. Steering the country's political compass through legislation, these two parties are intrinsic actors in American politics. Understanding their roles, policies, and how they shape the political climate are your first foot in the door to a political career. Now that you've seen the big picture, it's time to start pinpointing your political path. Ready to make your mark?

The Three Branches of Government

Before you plunge into the bounds of politics, it's crucial to thoroughly understand the U.S. political system especially its three branches namely: executive, legislative, and judicial. These are the fundamental components of the government's structure and each possesses unique, yet interconnected, functions and powers.

Firstly, let's talk about the executive branch. It's akin to the steering wheel of the nation, with the President as the captain. The President is not just a figurehead of the country but also a chief decision-maker. He or she is responsible for executing federal laws and heading international diplomacy. The Vice President, Cabinet, executive departments, and several independent agencies are the supporting cast in the executive branch, each playing a crucial role. Despite the immense power the President holds, remember it's not an absolute kind. Their decisions and actions are regularly checked and balanced by the other two branches.

These checks and balances ensure that no one branch becomes too powerful. It's a safeguard, a security mechanism that magnifies the democratic values the nation runs on. Winning an executive post, even on a local scale, can give you a phenomenal opportunity to shape policy and lead your community.

We then shift our focus to the legislative branch, the law-making body of the U.S. government. It consists of two houses, the Senate and the House of Representatives, often collectively referred to as the Congress. The primary role of this branch is to create and pass laws that govern the land. So if you've ever had a burning desire to rectify issues in your community through policy changes, the legislative branch presents an avenue to do just that.

The Senate comprises 100 members, with each state having two senators who serve a six-year term. Conversely, the House of Representatives is larger, with its members, referred to as congressmen or congresswomen, representing districts within states. The number of representatives for each state is based on its population, with a total of 435 representatives serving two-year terms. As a would-be political aspirant, let this illustrate the kind of impact you could wield in representing your constituents on a national stage.

The third branch of government is the judicial, which is essentially the backbone that supports and upholds the laws created by the legislative branch. It checks the constitutionality of laws and resolves legal disputes. The judicial branch is headed by the U.S. Supreme Court, with its nine justices appointed for life by the President with Senate approval. Lower federal courts, also included in the judicial branch, play crucial roles in administering justice and interpreting laws across the country.

Now, you might think that running for a position in the judicial branch is different. Indeed, it's not typically an area where elections come into play since appointments are made rather than elected. However, knowing how it works is important as the judiciary can directly affect policy and administration. The strength of political decisions often lies in their ability to withstand judicial scrutiny.

Another facet here is that many states elect judges for their state-level courts. So, if your background is in law, and you're more inclined towards justice than policy making or administration, serving in the judiciary can be an impactful manner to serve your community.

In combination, these three branches of government form a triune power mechanism that ensures the smooth functioning of the American democratic system. Grasping these core structures will improve your understanding and navigation of the political landscape.

While both the executive and legislative branches are significant to aspiring politicians, understanding the judiciary's role and powers can give you a pack of trump cards in the politics game. You will know how laws can be set into motion, how they can be executed, and how their validity is confirmed or quashed. It's all a grand balancing act.

Remember that knowing about the three branches isn't enough. It's the understanding of the interplay among these branches, the checks and balances, the subtleties of influence and power, that transforms a good politician into a great leader.

Ultimately, deciding where you fit best in this triumvirate of power is a personal call. Are you inclined toward the immediacy of action realized within the executive branch? Or is the law-making stature of the legislative branch more your speed? Perhaps, you're leaning towards upholding justice through the judiciary.

All three branches offer unique avenues to bring about the change you wish to see. Identify your strengths, ambitions, and passions, align those with an understanding of the three branches, and you're well on your way to carving a successful career in U.S. politics.

The Role of Political Parties

The foundations of U.S. political life are grounded in its two major political parties: Democratic and Republican. These parties play a crucial role in shaping the political landscape of the nation, and their influence extends far beyond merely nominating candidates for office.

So, how do these parties function and what's their role in the grand scheme of things? Well, political parties have a unique role in organizing and stimulating interest in public affairs. They provide a structure for political activists to participate in policy debates and to support preferred candidates.

Political parties, whether Democrat, Republican, or third party, structure the political dialogues in America. They organize public opinion in a way that supports the functioning of a democratic society; they group similar ideas and beliefs together, providing voters with a streamlined way to understand and engage with the range of opinions on various issues.

Political parties are also responsible for fielding candidates. They recruit, groom, and support individuals seeking office. These candidates typically espouse the party's platform or general policy positions, helping to further spread these ideas among the electorate.

Moreover, political parties provide a framework for governance. Legislators from the same party often work together on policy proposals and votes. This cooperation extends to the executive branch too, where presidents often select party members for key administration positions. It's this machinery that helps translate party ideas into actual policy.

We should also note the crucial role parties play in fostering political participation and engagement. By volunteering for a party, citizens learn about the political process and become active participants. Parties offer avenues for citizens to express their views, rally for their issues, and even take steps toward running for office themselves. This kind of engagement is vital for a healthy democratic society.

Also, political parties provide a sense of identity for many people. A party affiliation can be a powerful motivator and a way of aligning oneself with a particular group, ideology, or set of policies. It can drive people to take political action and can be a significant factor in how individuals vote.

In addition to the major parties, there are numerous third parties–the Libertarian Party, Green Party, Constitution Party, and others. They play their part in injecting different ideas into the political discourse. While they may not win many elections, their ideas can impact the national conversation and occasionally influence the platforms of the major parties.

While political parties in the United States play an essential role in representing the electorate and shaping policy, they're also a common source of public frustration. Partisan divides can lead to legislative gridlock, and some feel that the two-party system limits representation. That said, the influence and importance of these institutions are undeniable.

Now, the nuances between political parties aren't always black and white, they can be significantly different depending on the region or even at local levels. It's, therefore, essential to understand the local political climate and how it aligns or conflicts with the national party platform. This knowledge can inform your campaign strategy and help you tailor your message.

Last, but surely not least, you've got to understand that party loyalty is a heavy influencer in voting behavior. Not everyone reads up on every candidate. Some people vote strictly along party lines. So, choosing the right party can help sway voters in your favor – if their values align with yours, they'll likely pick you just because you're in the 'right' party.

Political parties aren't perfect, and they can certainly be a source of contention and frustration. But they're an integral part of how our democracy operates, and understanding their role and function is key to any political journey. So, whether you align yourself with a major party or wave the flag of a third party, understanding and leveraging the structure and influence of political parties is paramount to successful campaigning.

Simply put, political parties are much more than mascots at election time, they are machines with moving parts that shape the path of American politics and society. As you dive deeper into your political career, remember to navigate these political "tides" with perspective and grace. It's all part of the game, and it's a game you've decided to play.

Chapter 2:
Election Types in America

Just as your journey through the U.S political system continues, so does our discussion. We're headed right into the vital matter of election types. America doesn't have a one-size-fits-all voting process, and understanding the differences is key to formulating a successful campaign strategy. Starting at the top echelon, we have the presidential election, a national affair that occurs every four years. This is followed closely by the federal elections, comprising Senate and House of Representatives elections. Senators, 100 in total, serve staggered six-year terms, while the 435 representatives are up for election every two years. There's a dynamic chess game of strategy and positioning at play here, as new seats open and others are defended. Digging a layer deeper, we find the state elections. These occur for positions such as Governor or State Attorney and are crucial as they often have a more immediate impact on people's daily lives. And lastly, we reach the grassroots level - local elections. County commissioners, school board members, judges. Understanding these roles, and the people who inhabit them, can make a world of difference during your campaign. Strategically navigating these different election types will play a massive role in your political journey, so it's vital you can distinguish each one and recognize their unique opportunities and challenges.

Presidential Election

Ready to dive right into the biggest of them all? The Presidential Election? This is not for the faint-hearted. It's the Super Bowl of politics. The stakes are high and the competition is fierce. But if you're aiming for the top, you're in the right place.

First, let's talk about mechanics. The U.S. presidential election happens every four years on the first Tuesday of November. The process, though, begins much earlier. Candidates typically announce intentions to run for presidency one to two years before the election, allowing ample time for their team to build a campaign, garner funds, and gain voter support.

The competition within each political party usually begins with primaries and caucuses in the various states and territories. Much like a state championship where teams decide who gets to go to the nationals, a political party holds these preliminary contests to select the candidate who will be representing them in the presidential election.

Once each party's candidate is confirmed, they battle for voter support in an extensive campaign trail that includes public speaking engagements, media interviews, social media interactions, and more. This often grueling journey pits candidate against candidate until voters play their hand on Election Day.

Importantly, presidential elections aren't won by securing the majority of the popular vote. Instead, they're won through the Electoral College, a body of 538 delegates who cast electoral votes on behalf of their respective states. Candidates need to earn 270 electoral votes to claim victory.

Focusing on swing states, or battleground states as they are also called, can be a vital strategy. These states have a history of fluctuating between supporting Democratic and Republican party candidates. Winning in these states can tip the balance of the electoral votes in a candidate's favor.

While understanding the process and strategy is critical, so too is building a reliable, dedicated campaign team. A presidential hopeful needs a strong campaign manager and policy advisors, along with robust media and public relations strategies. You may not need to pack your team with big names, but you do need individuals who are knowledgeable, look out for your best interests, and command respect.

Loyalty is important but not the only prerequisite. Look for experienced individuals who can navigate the complex political landscape with agility and intelligence. They should have an excellent understanding of the prevailing sentiments in America and be capable of making strategic decisions based on this knowledge.

You'll also need a robust policy platform to present to voters. Articulating your political stance and plans clearly is key. Policies aren't just a list of proposals—you'll need to persuasively argue for your policies and address voters' concerns. Dissect prevailing issues and use insight-led, tailored, voter-centric content and communication to win hearts and minds.

Financing your campaign is another crucial aspect. The funds required to run a successful campaign can run into millions, if not billions. Learning about campaign finance laws and identifying potential donors to help fund your campaign will be a significant part of your journey to the Oval Office.

Beyond the money, you'll need grassroots mobilization to broaden your base. Think beyond social media fame—real-life networks, outreach programs, volunteer drives, and town hall meetings can enhance voter connection and translate to more support at the ballot box.

Finally, mastering public speaking is a must. From scripted speeches to off-the-cuff remarks to handling media interviews, your words will powerfully shape your campaign's narrative. It's okay to be nervous in the beginning, but with practice, you'll become a commanding speaker. Instead of fearing the microphone, use it as a powerful tool to communicate your ideas and inspire supporters.

All in all, running for the presidency requires intense preparation, but success can be achieved with a compelling vision, a capable team, robust support, and dogged resilience. Keep these fundamental elements in mind and you'll be well on your way to making a significant splash in the presidential pool.

Federal Elections

Now, let's discuss Federal elections. They're a different ball game compared to presidential races, and understanding the intricacies can put you in a powerful position. Divided into two main types–Senate and House of Representatives elections–they're held every two years on the first Tuesday in November. The Senate elections see a third of the seats up for grabs every two years, with members serving six-year terms. House elections, on the other hand, are a complete turnaround, with all 435 seats on the table every two years. You'll need to consider the breadth and depth of your voter base, given every state has just two Senators but varying numbers of Representatives depending on the state's population. So, does your appeal lie with your state at large or a specific Congressional district? A successful foray into Federal elections often requires different strategies, resources, and messaging compared to other election types. It's also imperative to appreciate the significant role these elections play in shaping national policy direction and the balance of power in Congress. You're not just running for an office; you're vying for a chance to effect tangible change on a national scale.

Senate Elections are among the most significant fixtures in the American political landscape, playing a pivotal role in shaping the country's future. The Senate is one of two chambers in the United States Congress, with the other being the House of Representatives. Consisting of 100 members, two from each state, the U.S. Senate is charged with duties that are critical to the running of the federal government.

Senators serve six-year terms with staggered elections, which means every two years, approximately one-third of the Senate is up for election. This unique mechanism ensures continuity and experience within the Senate. Unlike the House of Representatives, where the entire body is up for election at once, the Senate's structure ensures a level of stability and consistency.

Running a campaign for Senate is no small feat. It requires strategy, perseverance, and, yes, substantial financial resources. However, it's your vision and ability to resonate with voters that should be your greatest asset. The task may seem daunting, but with the right approach, you can craft a successful path towards your goal.

Start with building a robust team. Collaborate individuals who are passionate about your vision, competent, and willing to commit to the campaign's demands. While your team will consist of a range of experts, including financial advisors, political strategists, and communications specialists, it's crucial that everyone shares a common goal: to get you elected.

The next critical step is to establish a compelling political platform that aligns with the needs, values, and interests of your prospective constituents. Every voter group is different, therefore it's important to tailor your message to address their unique concerns and aspirations. Listening to these voters is key. Town halls, public forums, and community engagements are valuable avenues to understand their perspectives and incorporate them into your campaign strategy.

Funding is a practical aspect of the campaign that cannot be overlooked. Raising money for a Senate campaign involves navigating complex campaign finance laws and aggressively pursuing fundraising opportunities, while simultaneously aligning funding strategies with voter mobilization efforts. Remember, every dollar raised is a testament to the level of public support you've garnered.

Given the national weight that Senate elections carry, engaging with voters at the grassroots level can make a decisive difference. Knocking on doors, making phone calls, and leveraging digital platforms to reach voters are all integral parts of a successful campaign strategy. Taking time to personally relate to voters can build trust, respect, and a real sense of connection. This personal touch could tip the scales in your favor.

Public speaking is another crucial aspect of your campaign. The Senate's prestige demands articulate, informed, and persuasive speakers. Your speeches must resonate with voters, inspire trust, and emphasize the strength and vitality of your vision for the nation. Craft your speeches carefully and practice thoroughly. The ability to think on your feet and respond decisively during media interviews and debates will further differentiate you from your competition.

Debates often highlight critical moments in a campaign, underscoring the importance of preparation and strategy. Effective debaters know their material, anticipate opposition arguments, and can articulate clear, concise rebuttals. Practice, review, and refine your responses to tough questions. This will help you maintain control during the debate and navigate it with ease and confidence.

As the election day approaches, your campaign strategy should reach a crescendo. A final campaign push can consolidate support and generate momentum, crucial in securing victory. Plan for a comprehensive election day strategy, from securing the necessary poll workers to get-out-the-vote efforts, everything needs to be meticulously organized for the D-day.

After the election, take the time for a thorough post-election analysis. Win or lose, there are always lessons to be learned. What worked well? What needs improvement? Such self-reflection can lead to a greater understanding of the complexities of running a Senate campaign and prepare you better for future challenges.

Finally, be reminded of the profound responsibility attached to running for Senate. You're not just seeking an office, you're aspiring to be a representative of the people and wield influence on decisions of national importance. With the right preparation, commitment, and mindset, you can be the change you wish to see in the U.S. Senate. Now, it's time to get started!

House of Representatives Elections is a key focus section for anyone planning to make a splash in America's political ocean. These elections are a considerable part of the federal elections and offer a unique opportunity for individuals wanting to effect change and serve their communities while earning a broader national platform. By learning about how these elections work, you are one step closer to understanding how you can make an impact.

The House of Representatives, also known as the 'The House', is one of the two chambers of the United States Congress, the other being the Senate. It's important to recognize that the House is a vibrant and dynamic body, reflecting the diversity and dynamism of our country. Its seats are up for election every two years, meaning that its composition can quickly change. This fast turnaround lends it to be more responsive to the public mood.

These biannual elections for the house take place on the 'first Tuesday after the first Monday in November'. The frequency may seem overwhelming, but it's a shot at an effective public service or potential public policy change more often than the Senate or presidential elections.

Now, you might be wondering why these elections are of such significant importance. Well, the House of Representatives has the power to introduce revenue bills, impeach federal officials, and elect the President in case of an electoral college tie. And trust me, that's pretty substantial power. Therefore, winning a house election gives you the chance to shape national and economic policy fundamentally.

But before you jump in headfirst, understanding the fundamentals of eligibility is a must. The constitution mandates that members of the House must be at least 25 years old, been a U.S. citizen for at least seven years, and live in the state they represent. Interestingly, you don't necessarily have to live in the district you want to represent, albeit it is often seen as advantageous.

The structure of the House elections is fairly straightforward - highest number of votes wins. Unlike the Senate, there isn't a need to win a majority of votes,which certainly simplifies matters. However, competition for these seats is fierce, given the short two-year term, expect an intense and fiery campaign season.

On the topic of districts, understanding their role is vital. The House seats are divided among the states based on the population. Each state has a minimum of one representative, with the total number of representatives capped at 435. This information is crucial as you plan your election strategy – after all, the district's demographics will often inform your platform and the issues you decide to champion.

One crucial aspect of House elections you must be aware of is the process of redistricting. This refers to the redrawing of congressional districts after every decade, following the national Census. Redistricting can have a profound effect on House elections, not only by shifting boundaries but also by changing the demographic makeup of districts. Hence, staying on top of these changes can make all the difference in a tight race.

As for campaigning strategies, remember the magic word - local. Focus on local issues, local needs, tireless grassroots organizing, and direct voter contact. As a representative, your primary job will be to represent your constituents, and what better way to assure them you're their best choice than by showing a deep understanding of their concerns and aspirations?

Preparing for a primary is another significant factor in your house race journey. Primaries are the method political parties use to nominate their candidates for the general election, and they can be just as competitive. Make sure to utilize this as an opportunity to refine your message and build your campaign base.

When it comes to land a seat in the House,the importance of fundraising cannot be understated. Simply put, running a campaign is expensive. According to the Center for Responsive Politics, the average successful House campaign in 2018 cost about $2 million. This requires a strategic plan to secure the financial resources needed for your campaign's success.

Using social media platforms is an exceptional tool in this digital age. It increases your visibility, your chances of engaging with voters, and it's cost-efficient to boot. Yet it's important to balance this with traditional media outlets and boots-on-the-ground campaigning. Not all voters are active on social media, and despite this digital age, personal contact can leave a lasting impact.

All things considered, running for a seat in the House of Representatives is a rigorous yet rewarding process. It's a whirlwind of high stakes decisions, strategic plans, intense campaigning, and firm conviction in the values you represent. Ultimately, it offers the chance to serve constituents closely, influence national policy, and be a part of our country's vibrant democratic process.

Whether you are a political newcomer or a seasoned veteran, understanding House elections is vital in your journey towards victory. Equipped with this knowledge, a passion for public service, and the courage to leap, you are ready to step towards that laminate desk in D.C.

State Elections

Your venture into politics doesn't have to start at the top. Many influential politicians have made their mark through state elections. These elections are critical because state governments shape laws and policies affecting education, trade, public health, and environment, among others. With that in mind, let's delve into the specifics.

The structure of state government mirrors the federal system with executive, legislative, and judicial branches. As such, state elections encompass a wide range of positions – from the Governor to members of the state legislature, all the way down to various judgeships.

Let's start with arguably the most influential role at the state level, the Governor. Now, running for Governor isn't a walk in the park. It's an outstanding opportunity to implement meaningful change but also a high-stakes undertaking. A successful gubernatorial campaign requires a robust platform, a strong team, clear messaging, and significant resources for campaign funding. Hence, this role requires foresight, courage, and tenacity.

Alongside the gubernatorial office, we also have Lieutenant Governor's post, Secretary of State, Attorney General, and Treasurer or Comptroller's roles up for grabs in most states. While they may not come with as much prestige as the Governor's office, they're crucial in managing the state's activities and shaping local laws and policies.

The next part of the state election equation is the legislative branch. Much like the Federal Congress, each state has its legislature comprised of at least two chambers — the Senate and the House of Representatives. Running for a position in the state legislature is another excellent way to wade into the political sphere and make a tangible difference in your community.

Running for state legislative office requires an intimate understanding of the issues that matter to your district. It's about representing your constituents and making sure their needs and desires are reflected in the laws your state passes. In essence, you become a microcosm of the voice of the people, which is a powerful greenhouse for effective leadership.

Lastly, it's worth mentioning that judicial elections are also part of the state election process in many states. Depending on the state, you might find judgeships for the State Supreme Court, Appellate Court, and various Trial Courts. Running for judicial office requires not only legal expertise but your ability to communicate your ideals and principles to the electorate.

In terms of timing, state elections typically coincide with federal elections. Still, there can be variations. Some states have off-year elections, while others may schedule special elections in non-election years. Familiarizing yourself with the state's election calendar is essential to plan your campaign effectively.

State elections go beyond just the individuals running for office. They're about ballot measures, propositions, and amendments to the state constitution. Engaging in these aspects of state politics allows you to help shape your state's future directly.

Before embarking on a state election campaign, it's crucial to research state-specific election laws and regulations. Each state has its processes, deadlines, and rules regarding matters like campaign financing, ballot access, voter eligibility, and redistricting, which would inevitably affect your campaign strategy.

Running a successful state campaign requires a great deal of planning and preparation. Developing a keen sense of what voters care about most, identifying potential funding sources, building a strong volunteer base, managing a dedicated campaign team – these are just a few of the prerequisites to launching a winning state campaign.

Remember that your journey in state elections will offer many valuable lessons. There will be triumphs and setbacks, but each step is an opportunity to learn, grow, and refine your approach for the next hurdle. It's not an easy path, but with determination, focus, and savvy strategizing, you'll be well on your way to fostering change on a state level.

All in all, state elections provide a golden opportunity to make a meaningful impact on the lives of your fellow citizens. They're the backbone of our democracy – nurturing leaders, fostering change, and giving power to the people. So, don't overlook the potential that lies in state elections – you might just find it's the perfect stepping stone for your political journey!

Local Elections

As we continue from state elections, let's deep dive into local elections, arguably some of the most vital and impactful elections held in America today. Why so? Well, local elections have a direct influence on our day-to-day lives. They're the decisive factor in collective decisions about school leadership, public safety, infrastructure, and more. Setting your sights on local office could be an excellent choice for your political career, particularly if you're passionate about serving your immediate community.

Local elections encompass a gamut of public offices ranging from school boards to mayoralties, from county judges to city councils. These positions, though they might seem less glamorous compared to Congress or the Presidency, have tangible and immediate effects on constituents. Road repairs, local taxes, school district decisions – local officials call the shots on these issues.

But how does one approach local elections? Well, the rules and structure of local elections tend to vary by state, county, and city. It's crucial to thoroughly investigate the regulations that govern the specific office you're considering. Some cities elect mayors via direct, citywide elections, while in others, the city council elects the mayor internally.

Most local electoral races are nonpartisan, which means candidates do not officially represent a particular political party. Instead, these elections focus more on issues relevant to the local community. However, being aware of your constituents' party leanings won't hurt and could be a deciding factor in close races.

In local elections, having a strong, recognizable presence within the community is a significant advantage. Unlike federal or state elections, where aspects such as party affiliation and national politics play a bigger role, local elections tend to focus more on the candidate's character, trustworthiness, and connections.

When campaigning locally, it's essential to speak directly to the unique concerns and interests of your community. Tailoring your campaign message to reflect the needs of your constituents is critical. You'll want to highlight your commitment to local issues such as public safety, schools, and local economic development in a clear and compelling manner.

Building a Network is another key aspect of local elections. Cultivated associations with community leaders, local business owners, and constituents can take you far. Engaging with civic organizations, local businesses, and non-profit agencies can help you create a strong local network. Also, remember that even small events, like town fairs or school meetings, can be fantastic networking opportunities.

Local elections are often won on the ground, meaning door-to-door campaigning plays a significant role. This grassroots approach gives you an opportunity to personally appeal to voters, get a sense of the electorate's mood, and learn what issues are most important to them.

Offering hands-on solutions to local problems is the best way to win voters in local elections. Focus on actionable plans to improve local education, foster economic growth, maintain public safety, etc. Remember, you'll need to be able to deliver on your promises – local officeholders are directly accountable to their constituents. That accountability can be scary, but it's also an opportunity to really make a difference.

Local offices also require significantly less campaign funding compared to state or federal ones. As a result, fundraising for local elections is typically more attainable, focusing on small, individual donations from local community members. It's still vital to plan and organize your campaign budget carefully, as strategic allocation can help bolster your reach and success.

Social media can also play an essential role in local elections. Platforms like Facebook, Twitter, and Instagram allow you to connect directly with constituents, share your message, and build a strong online presence. In conjunction with traditional campaigning methods, an effective social media strategy can give you a significant edge in a local election.

Finally, remember that every election is a learning experience. Running for local office provides a real boots-on-the-ground view of the political process. You'll gain valuable experience in campaigning and governance that can set the stage for higher offices in the future, should you aspire to them.

In sum, local elections provide a unique opportunity for you to serve your community, build political experience, and make a real, palpable impact. Playing an essential role in improving your community is no small feat, and the rewards can outweigh any challenge you might face along the way.

Chapter 3:
Deciding Your Political
Career Direction

You've got a solid grasp on the structure of our U.S. political landscape, and you're familiarized with the array of election types. Now comes the formidable and admittedly, exciting task of honing in on your political career path. Think of it as navigating on a complex political map; you need to pinpoint your strengths, to know your true north. Are you a persuasive speaker? A skilled negotiator? Or perhaps you excel in building genuine connections with community members? Your unique talents will greatly inform your trajectory. On the other end, the choice of office is an equally core determinant. Be realistic about your experience and your resources, but also about what you aspire to achieve. Maybe your impact would be more profound on a local level? Or perhaps federal challenges call to your sense of duty? Choosing the right path is a balancing act, gluing together what you're good at, what you want, and where you're most needed. So, pull out that political compass, it's time to plot your course in the fascinating maze of American politics.

Analyzing Your Strengths

The realm of politics, like most pursuits, is better navigated if we first take the time to understand ourselves. It's beneficial to step back and analyze our strengths, considering how they can serve us in the political sphere. This doesn't merely pertain to your knowledge and technical skills, but also to your intrinsic attributes - the core qualities that make you unique.

First, let's explore those special characteristics that you bring to the table. Maybe you're an exceptional communicator who can seamlessly weave the most complex ideas into understandable narratives. Perhaps you have a knack for negotiation, a quality that is always welcomed in politics. You could even possess exceptional empathetic abilities, helping you to connect with a wide range of people and their problems. We all have something that sets us apart. The point is to identify those factors and bring them to the political battleground.

The question is, how do we define these strengths? Start by asking those who know you well – your friends, family, colleagues, mentors. Their perspectives can shine a light on attributes you might have overlooked or undervalued. Of course, their views should be taken as insights, not absolutes. You understand yourself best, but sometimes, an external perception can trigger introspection.

Another method is to reflect on your experiences. Consider the times when you felt most effective, potent, and fulfilled. There is a good chance these instances highlight your most integral strengths. They could be situations where you rallied people towards a cause, made a significant decision under pressure, or solved a complex problem. They can even be subtle moments of understanding and empathy.

While identifying your strengths is crucial, equally significant is understanding how each of them can be leveraged in your political journey. If you're a powerful public speaker, it may be worth considering roles that involve regular interactions with constituents or media. If, on the other hand, you thrive in behind-the-scenes strategic planning, roles that require policy development might be more suited to your abilities.

Let's say you've recognized that empathy is one of your standout qualities. Polished empathy can become your superpower as a politician. It can help you connect deeply with the electorate, understand their issues at a fundamental level, and communicate your sincerity and intention to work for the welfare of the people. You'd be surprised how much people appreciate feeling heard and understood - it's a key element in gaining their trust and respect.

Moreover, it's crucial to utilize your strengths to bridge gaps. Politics often entails disagreements and conflicts. Suppose your strength lies in negotiation and resolution. In that case, you can leverage that strength to bring people with diverse perspectives together, thus promoting unity and consensus-building for the collective good.

All this introspection doesn't mean that your strengths remain static throughout your political journey. They can change, develop, and grow with you. Our ability to adapt and learn is one of our most profound human qualities. So, even though it's essential to play to our strengths, it's equally crucial not to become too complacent or rigid. Flexibility can be an asset, especially in unpredictable environments.

Remember, strength doesn't imply a lack of weaknesses or areas for improvement. We all have areas where we can grow and evolve; acknowledging these shows humility and makes the process of learning new skills less daunting. Emphasizing strengths shouldn't keep us from improving in other aspects. Balance, as they say, is everything.

Next, don't hesitate to get training or advice on how to amplify your strengths. There are plenty of resources available, both online and offline, to refine and polish the skills you need in your political pursuits. This could include public speaking classes, negotiation workshops, or leadership seminars. Educational programs like political science or law can also offer beneficial formal training.

Finally, keep in mind that the journey is as important as the destination. Embrace opportunities to learn, grow and evolve. Politics, like every worthy pursuit, can be a path of personal development. Look at each experience - good or bad - as an opportunity to understand yourself better and become the most effective and empathetic political leader you can be.

By analyzing your strengths, you can effectively map out a path that aligns with your abilities and passions. In the end, it's not just about winning an election; it's about making a difference in the most impactful way that you can. Your strengths are your most valuable assets in this pursuit, and recognizing them is just the beginning.

Choosing the Right Office

So, we've done a bit of soul-searching and some serious self-assessment. You've brushed a spotlight over your skills and strengths, and now you have your political career direction at the helm of your thoughts. The next crucial step is determining which political office fits your political aspirations. A seemingly daunting decision, sure. But remember, it's not rocket science, and a thoughtful, careful analysis can take you down the right political lane.

First, consider the level of government you aspire to serve. In the United States, the political landscape is platted into federal, state, and local levels. Think of these different levels as a layered cake—a metaphor that can also apply to their complexity and size. Each layer presents unique opportunities, challenges, and responsibilities. The key lies in determining which level best aligns with your abilities, interests, and, of course, your ultimate goal.

If you are passionate about national issues, and believe that you can make a difference on a national scale, then perhaps the Federal level is for you. This would involve aiming for office in the House of Representatives or the Senate. But with great power comes great scrutiny. Federal level office demands rigorous campaigning and fundraising, as well as a firm and broad understanding of complex national issues.

However, if your interests tend more toward state-level matters, there are many roles you can consider, from the Governorship to a seat on the State Senate. Engaging with state-level politics can make a profound impact on your community, and the level of exposure, while conscious, is significantly less than that on a Federal level.

Moving onto the local layer, here's where the ingredient of personal connection flavors the mix. If your motivations are rooted in your local community and you thrive on close interactions with your neighbors, positions such as City Council, School Board, or Mayor may be right for you. Local offices offer a valuable stepping stone into politics and are often a nurturing ground for potential leaders.

Remember, choosing the right political office is, ideally, a combination of your passion, your abilities, and logically, where you see yourself fitting into the grand political puzzle. It is about reconciling what you want to achieve with the realities of what each position includes.

One significant factor to consider is the time commitment that each role demands. It varies significantly across positions and political levels. Local level offices usually maintain part-time roles, allowing for other professional engagements. However, a federal office role is a full-time commitment and then some more. Ensure you're ready to fully invest in your political ambitions, before you dive headfirst.

Another aspect to ponder upon is the inherent authority that each position holds. Some positions command more power than others. Ask yourself—is wielding power your main objective or is impacting policy more your speed? While this might sound a bit Machiavellian, understanding what you need out of your political journey can help narrow your options and clarify your decision-making process.

Also, be sure to explore the requirements for the role. Different political offices have varying eligibility criteria, including age, residency, and citizenship status. Consider these requirements right at the starting line to avoid any potential hurdles down the road.

When it comes to choosing the right office, there is no right or wrong answer, but rather what feels like the best fit for you. At the end of the day, whichever office you decide to run for should align with the change you aim to create, the audience you wish to serve, and the future you envision for yourself—and your fellow citizens. Running for office is a daunting task, but it's also an opportunity to influence the world for the better. Resist making a hasty decision.

Lastly, keep in mind that a political career often involves gradual progression. Rarely does one leapfrog to a high office without any prior experience. Welcome each opportunity as a stepping stone, a learning curve for the road ahead. Capitalize on each experience and use it as groundwork to catapult your career to greater heights.

In summation, choosing the right office is a critical and personal decision in your political journey. It requires introspection, focus, and a lot of groundwork. There might be uncertainties, and there will undoubtedly be challenges. But remember, success lies in turning stumbling blocks into stepping stones. So be brave, be patient, and stay committed to your course, remembering always that every great journey begins with a single step. Your political journey may indeed be a marathon, not a sprint, but with the right direction, perseverance, and more than a sprinkle of passion, the finish line may not be as far off as it seems.

Chapter 4:
Building Your Core Team

The heartbeat of your campaign rests directly in your core team. This ensemble of dedicated professionals is pivotal in turning your political dreams into realities. Like an orchestra conductor bringing together an arrangement of talents and expertise, your role in forming this team shouldn't be taken lightly. The Campaign Manager becomes your right hand person, essentially the CEO who ensures all parts of the campaign are moving smoothly, coordinating with other team members, volunteers and keeping you focused on your ultimate goal. Policy Advisors are the policy nerds, diving deep into the weeds of legislation and analysis, their expertise should align with your platform's issues, ensuring accurate, informed decisions. The roles of Media and Public Relations cannot be forgotten; your image, resonance with voters, and overall message largely rests in their hands. They not only deal with how you're presented, they manage potential crises and work diligently to enhance voter perception. This team is your lifeline, your brain trust, and your first line of defense. Building a strong, reliable, and efficient core team is the real first step on your political journey.

Role of the Campaign Manager

The campaign manager is the traffic control center of your political venture. They keep everything running smoothly, efficiently, and make sure everyone on the team knows their role. They're the ones who'll make sure your journey on the campaign trail doesn't hit unexpected road bumps, and if it does, they're more than capable of getting things back on track.

A campaign manager isn't just a manager in the traditional sense of the word. They are the strategist behind the chessboard, planning the campaign's every move. To make a mark in politics, you can't just make it up as you go. You need an articulate vision, detailed plans, and someone capable of executing them proficiently. That's where your campaign manager steps in.

One of the key duties of the campaign manager is to help determine the campaign strategy. This encompasses everything from identifying key voter demographics to outlining your stance on pivotal issues. They'll guide you on what neighborhoods to canvas, which community events to attend, and even what tone of voice to use when addressing certain topics. They have their finger on the pulse of the campaign, making decisions that will ultimately lead to success.

Organization is another paramount skill your campaign manager has to master. They'll keep track of critical dates like deadlines for filing, debate schedules, and important community events. They ensure that your schedule is manageable, that you're at the right place at the right time, and that all your legal and ethical obligations are met.

Campaign managers have a keen eye for the details and can discern where resources should be allocated for maximum impact. They'll assess whether it's more beneficial to invest in radio spots or Facebook ads, for example, and make budgetary decisions accordingly. In a world where resources are limited and competition is fierce, making smart decisions with where you pin your dollars is a crucial determinant of your campaign's success.

A campaign manager also has to build and maintain a well-oiled team. They select suitable staff for vital roles, from press secretaries to speechwriters, and make sure they're all working in harmony towards the shared goal. Ensuring effective internal communication and fostering a robust work ethic are significant parts of keeping the team together and motivated.

Another vital role of the campaign manager is to manage crisis situations. Campaigning isn't all sunshine and roses; rather, it's sure to face turbulence at times. In such instances, the campaign manager guides the team, navigating through any negative press or unforeseen incidences with skill and composure.

More than just a crisis manager, the campaign manager acts like a shield, protecting both the candidate and the campaign from potential harm. They closely monitor potential threats that could derail your campaign and come up with contingency plans to tackle them effectively.

Your campaign vision is the driving force behind your political race. Your campaign manager ensures this vision is properly articulated and communicated. They'll help you convey your ideology and goals coherently, ensuring your message resonates with the voting public.

It's also important for your campaign manager to have a great understanding of current affairs and voter sentiment. They need to be in tune with the American political climate and possess a deeper understanding of the electorate's needs and concerns. This knowledge helps to tailor your campaign narrative, engage with your constituents more effectively, and secure their votes.

Public relations management also falls within the remit of the campaign manager. They work closely with your communications team to steer public opinion and manage interactions with the media. They'll also supervise the production of campaign promotional material and maintain your public image.

The campaign manager's duties extend far beyond the candidate. They also interact closely with political party leaders and potential endorsers, keeping everyone aligned and drumming up additional support for your campaign.

Lastly, campaign managers provide moral support when the going gets tough. They're the ones who give you a pep talk, encourage you to keep going when the odds are stacked against you, and inspire the team to put their best foot forward.

In summary, your campaign manager is your right-hand person, your confidant, your chief strategist, and your crisis controller. When it comes to running a successful political campaign, the role of the campaign manager cannot be overstated.

Importance of Policy Advisors

The cornerstone of any successful political campaign is grounded in a thorough understanding of policy and the issues that matter most to voters. This is where policy advisors play an indispensable role. As their name suggests, they advise on policy, providing an essential insight into manifold areas from healthcare to tax reform and foreign policy.

Policy advisors are critical for shaping the backbone of your campaign. They dive deep into issues, lay out pros and cons, and inform the credible stance that molds into your political platform. Part of their duty is to act as your eyes and ears- they keep you updated on current trends, emerging issues, shifts in public opinion, and legislative changes that directly impact your political positioning.

Often, policy advisors use their knowledge and expertise in a specific issue area to help you craft compelling policy proposals that resonate with your voters. These specialists provide data-driven analysis and present you with information that puts you in the best position to make informed policy decisions. When you can relate facts to everyday people's lives- you've sparked a meaningful connection.

Think of policy advisors as navigators in the vast ocean of policy-making. They know how to translate convoluted policy language into the language of laymen. This ability to make complex issues accessible to the average voter is a key skill that helps win elections. The more your voters understand the issues, the better they can connect with your policy stance and electoral promise.

At the same time, policy advisors help you anticipate and counter arguments from political rivals. By knowing the ins and outs of a policy, and where your competitor stands, they'll arm you with rebuttals and counterpoints to stay ahead in debates and public discourse.

The role of these advisors extends beyond crafting policy. A seasoned advisor can advise you on communicating your policy stance strategically. They understand the subtlety of framing your position rightly, spinning an unanticipated policy event, or choosing the right moment to announce a critical policy proposition.

Policy advisors also help gauge potential weaknesses in your policy stance. If there's a possibility that your stance on an issue could alienate a segment of voters, they'll be the first to uncover it. Together, you can figure out how to approach this sensitive matter, ensuring that your campaign retains its broad appeal.

Given their broad responsibilities, it's not surprising that having an experienced and knowledgeable policy advisor is as important as it is. You need someone who can not only dissect and interpret policy accurately but can also keep a pulse on the prevailing moods, sentiments, and undercurrents among various voter demographics.

In the hustle and bustle of your campaign, policy advisors are your anchorage, keeping you grounded to the hard facts and offering a reality check when needed. They challenge your assumptions, present different perspectives, and ensure your policy strategies are rooted in reality.

Now, you might ask- how many policy advisors do you need? The answer depends on the scale and scope of your campaign. For a local election, one or two experienced advisors might suffice. If you're running for state or federal office, you'll need a team of advisors, each specialized in different policy areas, to provide you a comprehensive understanding.

Selecting your policy advisors should be a thoughtful process. Look for individuals who not only have expertise in their respective areas, but also share your beliefs and core principles. Having a team that genuinely believes in your political vision makes a difference.

Finally, remember to maintain open lines of communication with your policy advisors. They are there to guide you, and their advice can help make the difference between a tight race and a successful campaign. Keep them close, listen to their perspectives, discuss disagreements openly, and appreciate their counsel.

Policy advisors are the cerebral power of your political machine. Their role is instrumental in defining your campaign, shaping your political persona, connecting with your voters and, in turn, moving closer to victory. Choose them wisely and let them guide you in steering your campaign on the path of success.

Importance of Media and Public Relations

Now that we've tackled the importance of having a stellar campaign manager and insightful policy advisors, let's zoom into the critical role that media and public relations play in your campaign. In fact, effective media relations are as vital as crafting the right policies. In a political landscape where public perception can make or break a campaign, you simply can't underestimate its impact.

Media, an umbrella term encompassing everything from newspapers to television and social media platforms, magnifies your message out to the world, acting as a bridge between you and the public. PR experts are the architects that build and maintain this bridge, ensuring that your message is communicated accurately, empathetically, and effectively.

The first key to mastering media and PR relations is understanding their role. They aren't just channels to broadcast your content; they're powerful tools to engage your audience, provoke thought, and encourage discussion. In the world of politics, you're not selling a product; you're championing an idea, a vision, and the media serves as an involvement platform, not just a transmission line.

So, let's start with television, still a significant source of news for many Americans. Despite the rise of social media, TV remains an influential platform for political campaigns. Whether it's a televised debate, a news interview, or a campaign ad during prime time, don't overlook the power of television to humanize your campaign, demonstrate your leadership, and reach a wide audience.

However, traditional media outlets like TV are just the beginning. Today, digital media holds an influential spot, largely due to its accessibility, speed, and broad reach. Platforms like Twitter, Facebook, and Instagram provide instant communication tools that allow campaigns to reach potential voters in previously unattainable ways. A well-placed tweet or impactful Instagram post can reach millions in a matter of seconds. But with great power comes great responsibility - misuse can lead to public backlash or worse, campaign derailment.

Your public relations arm needs to formulate a clear and strategic social media design, focusing not just on bulk posting, but also on engagement plans and damage control strategies. Consistent messaging, preventive monitoring, direct engagement, and swiftness in addressing concerns are key factors in social media success.

Print media, often overlooked in the digital age, is still valuable in shaping public opinion. Newspapers and magazines can drive in-depth coverage of your campaign, allowing for detailed discussions on your policies and vision. They're excellent vehicles for reaching specific demographics and geographic areas, and shouldn't be forgotten in your media relations strategy.

Radio, too, can serve as an effective communication tool. It offers a unique mix of personal touch and broad reach, excellent for reaching audiences during commutes or breaks, and for discussing issues in a bit more depth.

Managing all these communication channels may seem daunting, but that's what your PR team is for. Experienced PR professionals help to shape your image, manage your message, and respond to any potential crises that might arise during your campaign. They're your brand guardians, ensuring that your campaign projects a consistent, authentic and attractive image.

Ultimately, your goal is to build a genuine relationship with your audience. This connection should be based on trust, transparency, and shared values. Your PR team will guide you in slowing down, listening to your constituents, acknowledging their concerns, and responding thoughtfully.

Remember, it's not just about getting your message out, but also about understanding what the public says back. Monitor social media conversations, track letter to the editor sections in local newspapers, watch public opinion polls closely, and most of all, listen actively to feedback whenever you speak directly to constituents. This two-way communication will help underscore the importance of your constituents in your campaign, making them feel valued and heard.

Indeed, the importance of media and public relations in your political campaign cannot be overstated. They play a decisive role in shaping your campaign's image, amplifying your voice, reaching targeted voters, and creating an environment for winning campaigns. So, as you move forward with building your core team, make sure to give ample focus on recruiting experienced PR professionals and strategizing your media relations. After all, a campaign with a clear message that resonates with voters is a campaign headed for victory.

In the next section, we'll delve deep into the key aspects of developing your political platform, another arena where your media and public relations strategies will be of paramount importance. Stay tuned.

Chapter 5:
Developing Your Political Platform

A pivotal element to all this running-for-office business is defining your political platform. This is your ticket to connectedness, where you'll venture into the minds of the voters to comprehend their desires and needs. We're talking mainstream issues, from healthcare to taxes to foreign policy. But don't just regurgitate the popular tune; you've got to inject your own unique, authentic values into the mix. Think of it as the movie trailer for your political brand; it's got to be hard-hitting enough to capture attention and clear enough to convey your storyline. But remember, your platform isn't a wish-list of rainbow-themed promises. It's a pledge of practical steps you intend to take in order to represent voter interests. Here's a crucial takeaway - clear, concrete, credible. That's the potency-your-platform-needs mantra. It's not about telling folks what you think they want to hear. It's about engaging in a conversation, listening, and committing to action. It's about demonstrating that you're the real deal. So, go ahead, take one giant leap into the world of voters, building a platform that not just resonifies, but revolutionizes.

Understanding Mainstream Issues

Entering the realm of politics requires a comprehensive awareness of mainstream issues. These topics, which hold public interest and remain prominent in societal conversations, will form the crux of your political platform. So, it's imperative to stay abreast with developments and form informed, nuanced opinions.

The most effective politicians are empathetic listeners who can tap into the public sentiment, discern the critical issues, and sympathize with differing perspectives. While staying rooted in your views, understand that open-mindedness is indispensable to perceive the broader societal context. Engaging with others in respectful debate and deliberations often unearths aspects you might not have otherwise considered.

With mainstream issues often being multifaceted, don't fall into the trap of oversimplifying or resorting to populist sentiments just to gain a quick win. While it may be tempting to resonate with the masses, it's not prudent to compromise on policy complexities. Distinguish yourself as a well-informed and thoughtful public figure, rather than a demagogue promoting oversimplified solutions.

One must also consider the changing nature of mainstream issues. Topics such as healthcare, education, and economic policy have always been at the core of our political conversation, but issues such as climate change and technology's role in society have risen to prominence in recent decades.

Reflect upon how these changes have impacted the U.S. political landscape and your constituents. Understand that cultural shifts have seen issues such as civil rights, gender equality, and identity politics turn into significant mainstream topics. Timeless issues take on fresh nuances as circumstances evolve, so strive to see the bigger picture and adapt your stance accordingly.

Despite the significance of national issues, remember that your constituents will also turn to you for local concerns. Infrastructure, local taxes, public safety, and more can become mainstream topics within the context of your geographical domain. Nurture a profound understanding of these issues, for they will affect your electorate's daily life directly and substantially.

Beyond understanding these issues, it also pays to reflect on their root causes and cascading effects. For instance, while tackling homelessness, consider its underlying issues like affordable housing shortage, unemployment, mental health problems, and more. By unravelling these threads, you can approach mainstream issues with rich, broad, and beneficial perspectives.

Keeping abreast with mainstream issues necessitates dedication to ongoing learning and growth. Keep your finger on the pulse by reading widely across an array of news outlets, attending community meetings, and engaging in discussions with your constituents. Don't hesitate to reach out to experts for their insights, as they may provide invaluable perspectives on complex issues.

As a public figure, your viewpoints on mainstream issues will inevitably be under public scrutiny. Therefore, it's vital to justify your viewpoints with evidence-based arguments. Good politicians utilize data, research, case studies, and expert opinions to bolster their stance and inspire confidence in their leadership capabilities.

The most compelling political platforms are those that translate understanding of mainstream issues into actionable solutions. So, while learning about these issues, also brainstorm ways to address them efficiently and effectively. Tangible solutions will demonstrate your commitment to change and your ability to utilize your political power effectively.

Your understanding of mainstream issues will define your political narrative and your platform's credibility. Therefore, pursue the accuracy and depth of understanding with vigor. Don't merely shadow public sentiment; instead, strive to shape it by providing informed perspectives and leading constructive conversations about solutions.

As you journey through your political career, remember that understanding mainstream issues isn't a one-and-done task. It requires continual effort and adaptability. As the world evolves, so does the spectrum of mainstream issues. Staying abreast of these changes will ensure that your platform remains relevant, resonating with the collective consciousness and concerns of your constituents.

In conclusion, understanding mainstream issues is a critical aspect of shaping a compelling political platform. It requires keeping abreast of evolving societal conversations, understanding original and evolving nuances, and translating this knowledge into impactful policies and strategies. The art of politics, after all, is the art of understanding problems and crafting solutions that resound with those whose cause you serve.

Representing Voter Interests

Your journey towards running for office is rapidly advancing. You've understood the U.S. political system, decided your political career direction, built your core team, and begun the process of carving out your political platform. Now, it's time to dive into a crucial aspect of your campaign: representing voter interests.

Mapping out the interests of your prospective voters is a complex, but rewarding process. You're not just aiming to be the voice of those constituents; you need to deliver solutions that are significant, and policies that resonate with them.

First step: Know your constituents. Grab some reliable data. Delve into demographics, education levels, job industries, incomes, social issues, and more. Reading census data, conducting surveys, and even hosting town halls can enable you to truly understand your constituency. This process isn't a one-and-done; it's a continuous effort that requires you to stay connected with your voters' evolving needs and aspirations.

Secondly, let's talk about developing empathy. Genuine, powerful empathy. Don't just understand your voters, feel with them. Develop a deep, sincere understanding of the issues that affect them. Share in their joys, fears, concerns, and triumphs. Remember, a politician's job is more than legislating, it's about giving a voice to the voiceless and providing hope where it's lacking.

Thirdly, formulate actionable policies based on your voters' interests. All the empathy in the world means little if it doesn't translate into action. Voters want to know how you plan to solve their problems. Translate their needs into viable, realistic policies that address their concerns in practical ways. Remember, the promises you make have real-world implications for those you seek to represent.

It's also essential to communicate effectively. It's critical to articulate your understanding of voters' interests and concerns. Use every medium at your disposal: speeches, social media, town hall meetings, advertising, etc., to assure your constituents you understand their needs and are prepared to address them.

However, on your path to becoming an elected official, expect a diverse range of voter interests. Some people might prioritize healthcare, while others may focus on education, jobs, or law enforcement. Aligning your campaign with these various interests could seem daunting. That's where the art of negotiation comes in.

Some see politics as an arena for power moves; I encourage you to see it as a dance of diplomacy. Your constituents will have conflicting interests that you will need to balance. Learn to listen to all sides, give everyone a fair hearing, and then make policy decisions that serve the common good.

Representing voter interests isn't just about local issues. Especially if you're running for a role at the state or national level, you need to show that you can put local interests within the broader context of national and international policy. This is a delicate act of balancing the micro and the macro, the individual and the community, the local and the global. It's challenging, but then again, nobody claimed politics was easy!

Now here's an important policy tip: Avoid partisanship when it comes to voter interests. It's true that party loyalty is often a significant part of your political identity. But when it comes to serving your constituents, leave labels at the door. This is about serving the people, not party agenda.

It's also helpful to stay adaptable. Voter interests evolve, as do societal norms and political landscapes. Be ready to embrace change and learn along the way. Keep tracking your voters' interests and reformulate your stances and strategies as needed. Politics is about navigating the tides, not fighting against them.

Commit yourself to transparency. Share your decisions, the dilemmas you faced, the trade-offs you made. When voters are included in the process, they are more likely to understand and support your choices.

When you commit yourself to represent voter interests genuinely, your political career will have a strong foundation. You'll be a politician who stands for something, whose platform reflects the vox populi, the voice of the people. And isn't that what politics is really about?

Remember, you're in this to make a difference – to champion the needs of the people who place their hopes in your hands. Carry that belief in every policy decision, in every campaigning speech, in every voter interaction. Representing voter interests means doing the hard work to maintain trust, actively heed concerns, and deliver solutions.

So continue to march forward. Gather data, empathize, strategize, communicate well, and keep learning. Representing voter interests is the heart of every successful campaign, and your dedication to this process will undoubtedly reflect in your rising political career.

Chapter 6:
Campaign Fundraising

The power of campaign fundraising is undeniable, with sufficient funds being a critical factor in the success of any political campaign. It's more than just the resource to propel your leaflets into mailboxes and your advertisements onto airwaves, it's a public display of your supporters' confidence in your capability to represent them. To that end, it's pivotal to understand campaign finance laws. These laws, complex as they may be, exist to ensure transparency and promote fairness in the campaign process. Violations, whether accidental or intentional, can be catastrophic and tarnish your reputation. Don't let the rules intimidate you, instead view them as the necessary guidelines in your fundraising journey. Identifying donors and holding fundraisers is the core of campaign funding. Whether it's knocking on doors for small contributions, or courting wealthy individuals and political action committees for larger sums, it's all about relationship building. Don't hesitate to invest time in getting to know potential donors and communication is key in these relationships. Honor your commitments and show appreciation for all contributions, regardless of size. Remember, every dollar counts, and your objective is to generate funds and win the belief of voters in your capability to lead.

Understanding Campaign Finance Laws

The campaign finance laws in the United States are complex and ever-evolving. It's an unavoidable part of running for office, so wrapping your head around these laws can make a massive difference in your campaign's success. Understanding these laws will ensure you operate within legal bounds while maximizing campaign funding opportunities.

Substantial financial resources are often required to fund the various components of a campaign, including hiring staff, purchasing political advertisements, organizing rallies, and more. Therefore, having a comprehensive understanding of the financial aspects of a campaign, particularly campaign finance laws, is essential for any aspiring politician.

Historically, the Federal Election Campaign Act (FECA) governs campaign finance laws at the national level. Passed in 1971 and significantly amended in 1974, 1976, and 1979, this legislation regulates the conduct of political campaigns and outlines the rules around sourcing and using campaign funds. The FECA also established the Federal Election Commission (FEC) to enforce the nation's campaign finance laws.

One of the primary functions of the FEC is to control the amount of money that individuals and organizations can contribute to political campaigns. These are referred to as 'contribution limits' and are fundamental to understanding campaign finance laws. For individuals contributing to campaigns, the limit is currently set at $2,900 per election cycle.

On the other hand, organizations, such as Political Action Committees (PACs), can contribute up to $5,000 per election. There are also Super PACs, which have no contribution limits but carry strict rules concerning direct interactions with candidate campaigns.

Besides controlling contributions, the FEC mandates that all campaigns disclose the details of their financial transactions. This means that the public has the right to know who is funding a campaign, highlighting the importance of transparency in the campaign process.

But the FECA is not the only important regulation when it comes to campaign finance; the Bipartisan Campaign Reform Act (BCRA) of 2002, often referred to as the McCain-Feingold Act, brought significant changes to campaign finance law. The Act was designed to curb the influence of big money in politics by introducing restrictions on 'soft money' (unregulated contributions to political parties) and regulating 'issue advocacy ads'.

This law significantly impacted the fundraising strategies of many campaigns. In fact, many argue that these regulations, among others, gave birth to the modern digital fundraising strategy, particularly the increased focus on small, individual donations. Given the landscape of today's political campaigns, understanding the implications and limitations set by the BCRA is crucial.

It's also important to know about regulations for 'dark money,' particularly after the landmark Supreme Court case, Citizens United v. FEC in 2010. This ruling allowed corporations and unions to spend unlimited amounts in elections. The cash generally funnel through non-profit organizations that are not required to disclose their donors, hence 'dark money.'

As a future candidate, being aware of these laws is more than just legal compliance. It provides you with insights into your strategies for raising funds and allows you to plan your campaign wisely.

At the state and local level, campaign finance laws can differ widely. These laws can control who can donate money, how much they can donate, and how campaign funds can be used. Therefore, it's critical to explore and familiarize yourself with these laws when considering a run for state or local office.

The consequences for violating campaign finance laws are severe. Not only can violations lead to fines or even jail time for serious offenses, but they can also cause irreparable damage to your reputation and the trust that voters have in you.

Lastly, remember that education is a continuous process. The arena of campaign finance laws is frequently changing due to new legal rulings and legislation. Therefore, staying updated and consulting with a campaign attorney who specializes in campaign finance laws can go a long way towards ensuring your campaign's legal and financial security.

Having a grasp of campaign finance laws might seem daunting at first, but with a thorough understanding comes a lucrative fundraising strategy that respects legal boundaries and maintains voter trust. A combination of persistence, transparency, and compliance will provide a good foundation for a successful campaign.

Identifying Donors and Holding Fundraisers

Having a firm grasp on campaign finance laws is crucial in running a successful political campaign, but it's equally important to master the art of fundraising. This process includes two significant steps: first, you need to identify potential donors who'll support your campaign financially, and second, you need to hold efficient and compelling fundraising events. So let's get into the nitty-gritty of these crucial aspects of your campaign.

Properly identifying potential donors doesn't necessarily involve trying to rub elbows with the filthy rich or the super affluent. Early in the fundraising process, start by looking at those who are close to you – your friends, family, colleagues, and neighbors. These individuals, who know you and trust in your abilities, can be your first donor base. They can contribute not just money, but also their time, resources, and potentially valuable connections.

Branching out from this initial pool, begin to explore local businesses and community leaders. Demonstrating to them how your political platform benefits their interests could entice them to donate to your cause. The idea here is to form a connection, a partnership of sorts, based on shared interests and common goals.

From here, you can start reaching out to broader segments of the community. Work luncheons, networking events or community gatherings can be prime opportunities to meet potential donors. Show your dedication to the community's issues. Show who you are and what you stand for. Make them believe in you enough to invest in you.

Don't forget about utilizing the digital sphere for potential donors. Social media, mailing lists, and online platforms can connect you to people who may share your political values but aren't in your immediate vicinity. Make the most of these resources.

As you continue to identify donors, keep track of your efforts. Utilize a donor management system to keep all of your information handy. A good database will keep track of your contacts, interactions, and donations, helping you stay organized and efficient.

Once you've identified potential donors, it's time to shift your focus towards fundraising events. These are essential for bolstering your campaign funds, but more than that, they're an opportunity to showcase your platform, demonstrate your speaking prowess, and engage with potential voters.

For starters, consider hosting smaller, more intimate gatherings that allow potential donors to engage with you on a personal level. These can be anything from a dinner party at a supporter's home to a small community meet and greet. This type of event can provide a more relaxed setting to speak with individuals about your platform and hear their concerns one-on-one.

As your campaign progresses, you'll want to move on to larger and more formal fundraising efforts. Galas, silent auctions, themed parties – these types of events can draw a bigger crowd and therefore raise more money.

Please don't skimp on the planning phase. The key to a lucrative and successful fundraising event is to plan meticulously and promote aggressively. Draft a detailed roadmap for the event, from creating guest lists to organizing the evening's entertainment. Promote your event across all of your platforms, ensuring that your supporters know about it well in advance, and keep them posted with any updates.

No matter the size or formality of your event, it must be engaging. Remember, people are more likely to donate when they're moved by what you have to say. Fire them up with your speeches, ignite their passion for the cause, and they'll feel more inclined to open their wallets.

Also, don't forget to follow-up after the event. Thank your attendees for coming, perhaps with a personalized note, and offer them ways to stay engaged with your campaign. Building relationships with donors doesn't end after a donation is made; nurturing these relationships can lead to continued support.

Finally, keep in mind that fundraising isn't just about the money; it's about people. It isn't a transaction, it's a conversation. It's about connecting with individuals, understanding their concerns, hearing their opinions. It's about making them feel invested in your campaign and inspiring them to support your vision.

Mastering the ability to identify potential donors and hold successful fundraising events can end up being a pivotal part of your campaign. And remember, the core of it all is authenticity. When you are enthused about your cause, it will shine through, attracting supporters and their financial backing.

Chapter 7:
Building Voter Support

Now that we've covered the basis for how to fund your campaign and have a grip on your campaign finance laws, let's explore the crucial task of building voter support. Remember, it's the voters who'll ultimately influence your ascension to office, so sparking a connection with them holds paramount importance. The three main areas to focus on are effective voter outreach strategies, getting boots on the ground through grassroots mobilization, and making the most out of social media's immense power. With these strategies, you'll be informed, influential, and intimately connected with the people whose needs you want to represent. Inspire them, impassion them, and engage them at a human level. Personalized, tailored messaging will always win votes over general, one-size-fits-all communication. In the same vein, don't forget about grassroots mobilization. Sway public opinion from the bottom up: recruit enthusiastic volunteers, canvas neighborhoods, and rally locals for support. Last but not least, don't underestimate the power of the digitized world. Harness social media to cultivate an online presence that reaches wider audiences, facilitates real-time updates, and enables practical two-way communication. But remember, while digital outreach is a robust tool, it's also a double-edged sword. Ensure the messages sent online align with your campaign's values and maintain a consistent, reputable presence. Now, excavate every ounce of charisma within yourself as we prepare for the next chapter: mastering public speaking.

Effective Voter Outreach Strategies

As you transition from building your core team to actively engaging with the voting community, understanding and implementing effective voter outreach strategies becomes pivotal. This process involves not just reaching out to the larger voting public, but also connecting with them in meaningful ways that to gain their support and trust.

First and foremost, any voter outreach strategy should be grounded in a genuine respect for the electorate and a clear understanding of their needs and aspirations. If you can't connect and empathize with the voters, you won't be able to persuade them to back you up. So, it's crucial to keep your ears to the ground, get to know what matters most to the voters, and actively relate those concerns back to your campaign's messaging.

Having face-to-face interactions with voters is one of the most powerful ways to build a strong rapport. It's not just about knocking on doors; it also involves attending local events, participating in community meetings, and hosting your own events where you can engage directly with the electorate. Offer voters a platform where they can voice their concerns and get to know you on a personal level. Remember, showing up is half the battle.

Every good campaign should have an efficient way to track and follow-up with potential supporters. This is where having a strong voter database comes in. Utilize systems to track your interactions with voters and their responses. When you make personalized follow-ups, it signifies to the voter that their opinion is valued, which works wonders to lean their support towards you.

Voter outreach also involves providing clear, accessible information about how and where to vote. Don't assume that everyone knows the voting process. Make it a point to educate potential voters about voter registration deadlines, polling locations, and methods of voting. This will not only empower citizens with the ease of voting but also associate your campaign with empowering voter narratives.

Additionally, a successful outreach strategy is one that understands and engages with the diversity of the voter base. Don't limit your campaign to a single demographic. Reach out to different communities, engage in multilingual outreach and ensure your campaign's messaging resonates across different socio-economic backgrounds.

More than just diversity, inclusivity should be at the heart of your outreach strategy. Whether it's making your campaign events accessible to people with disabilities, advocating for the rights of marginalized communities, or ensuring your campaign staff reflects the diversity of the electorate - an inclusive campaign is one that is truly representative, and voters will notice this.

Consider also the power of partnerships in extending your campaign's reach. These could be with local businesses, community organizations, labor unions, or other groups that share a common cause with your campaign. By aligning with these groups, you can tap into existing networks of individuals who might be engaged and persuaded to support your candidacy.

A robust voter outreach strategy also requires a solid volunteer infrastructure. Volunteers can help with door-knocking, making phone calls, assisting at events, and spreading the word about your campaign in their circles. Encourage your supporters to get involved—not only can this amplify your outreach efforts, but it also instills a sense of ownership and engagement among your supporters.

The power of digital outreach in today's socio-political climate can't be overstated. Harnessing the capabilities of social media platforms, email newsletters, and online forums can help you reach a broad audience quickly and cost-effectively. Building a strong online presence also allows for easier sharing of campaign messages and voter engagement in online social spaces.

Interactive methods of outreach can also create a buzz around your campaign. This could take the form of town halls, Q&A sessions, webinars, live-streamed events, or online debates. Such interactive platforms allow for real-time engagement and provide voters the opportunity to engage directly with you and your campaign.

Virtual phone banking is another valuable tool for reaching out to voters, especially during times of social distancing. By using a cloud-based phone banking software, campaign volunteers can make calls to potential voters from the comfort of their homes. It's a great way to have personalized conversations with voters without geographical constraints.

Lastly, never underestimate the power of traditional media. Interviews, op-eds, and profiles in local newspapers or on local radio and television stations can be incredibly influential in reaching voters, particularly those who are less active on social media or online spaces.

Ultimately, the effectiveness of your voter outreach strategy will come down to the relationships you build with the voters. Your intention should be engaging voters in meaningful conversations, not just selling them your candidature. Remember, at the end of the day, politics is about the people. Show them you care, and they will stand by you.

Grassroots Mobilization

No matter the size of your campaign, harnessing the power of grassroots mobilization can make a big difference in your success. Utilizing this approach doesn't just get the word out about your candidacy; it can help build enthusiasm among voters and generate genuine support.

At the heart of a grassroots approach are your volunteers. These are your foot soldiers who will knock on doors, make phone calls, and participate in visibility events like rallies or parades. They help to spread your message to the community and create a personal connection with voters. It's important to communicate regularly with your volunteers, offer training and resources, and always express your appreciation for their efforts.

Consider establishing a volunteer leadership structure with dedicated individuals responsible for coordinating in specific regions or neighborhoods. This decentralizes the pressure and ensures there are localized leaders supporting the overall goal. This approach also makes large campaign tasks more manageable and increases the campaign's presence in local communities.

The cornerstone of any grassroots campaign is door-to-door canvassing. Going door-to-door to engage with voters is one of the most effective ways to get out your message. Personal interaction creates a bond and a degree of trust between the campaign and the electorate.

When it comes to door-to-door outreach, it is vital to be prepared, respectful, and concise. Ensure that you or your volunteers are familiar with your platform and can clearly articulate key points. Listening is just as important as talking during these exchanges. Remember, you are building a relationship with the voters.

Phone call efforts, or phone banking, is another fundamental aspect of grassroots mobilization. The aim is to reach as many people as possible, inform them about your campaign, and ask for their support. Training is crucial to make your phone banking efforts effective. Equip your volunteers with the necessary skills and a script as a guide, although personalized conversations will always have the greatest impact.

Visibility events like rallies, town halls, and parades offer another unique opportunity to interact directly with voters. They provide a platform to deliver speeches, engage with the community, and demonstrate your authenticity. Your visibility at these events also shows your commitment and dedication to serving the community.

A common mistake that many campaigns make is ignoring small-scale, personal events. House parties, for example, are an excellent and intimate way to engage directly with voters, answer their questions, and discuss issues that matter to them in a relaxed environment. Encourage your supporters to host these events and extend invitations to their network.

Successful grassroots mobilization also involves partnership with local organizations. Develop relationships with community and neighborhood groups, schools, non-profits, and local businesses. These connections will not only extend your reach but will also lend credibility to your campaign.

The rise of digital platforms offers additional opportunities for grassroots engagement. Emails, social media platforms, and virtual meetings are all tools that can help amplify your message. They offer a cost-efficient way to reach larger audiences quickly. However, be wary of relying solely on digital outreach. The most effective campaigns use both digital and traditional grassroots strategies in tandem.

No grassroots campaign would be complete without voter registration drives. Increasing the number of registered voters who support your platform can make a significant difference, especially in close races. Ensure you have a concerted plan to register new voters and remind them of upcoming elections.

Remember that grassroots campaigns are focused on the ground level. It's there that voter interactions happen; it's there that connections are built. Engage genuinely with the electorate about their concerns, your political platform, and how you envision creating change. This will create a dedicated supporter base that is highly motivated to cast their vote for you.

Running for office is no easy task, and grassroots mobilization is no exception. It requires commitment, strategic planning, and a lot of hard work. But if done right, grassroots campaigns can build remarkable momentum and community support that leads to successful election results. Utilize your supporters, leverage community relationships, and remain committed to engaging genuinely on the ground level, and you'll be well on your way to winning your election.

Consider grassroots mobilization as not just a tactic, but an embodiment of democratic principles. It is about making politics accessible, engaging communities, and emphasizing that every individual has a role in shaping their government. Without it, campaigns and politicians risk losing touch with the electorate, and the very people they strive to represent. So go out, knock on doors, make calls, attend events, and see the power of the grassroots movement work for your campaign!

Harnessing the Power of Social Media

As we dive deeper into the digital age, it's become increasingly important to understand and effectively utilize the power of social media in your campaign. This isn't a fringe strategy anymore - it's often the beating heart of voter engagement, the bloodstream of your campaign's message.

Social media platforms like Facebook, Twitter, Instagram, YouTube, Snapchat, and LinkedIn, are powerful tools for reaching your voters, especially the younger demographics. Not only do these platforms allow you to transmit your message directly to your audience, but they facilitate conversation with and between your supporters.

The first step to utilizing social media for your campaign is setting up and managing your online presence. Ensure you have a professional and updated profile across all major platforms. Remember, consistency is key. Use the same campaign logo, colors, and catchphrases across all platforms to create a strong, recognizable brand identity.

Next is content creation. The real power of social media comes from its ability to amplify your message so it reaches corners of your constituents you can't physically get to. Post frequently and consistently, sharing not only political messages and campaign updates, but also behind-the-scenes glimpses, personal anecdotes, and campaign event invitations.

A key element of social media is interactivity. It's a two-way street. Your followers want to feel heard and valued. Respond to comments, like posts, and involve your followers in conversation. Many campaigns have had success with Q&A sessions and town halls hosted on these platforms. Your aim should always be to spark a dialogue and engagement, rather than simply broadcasting your message.

Another powerful aspect of social media is the ability to rapidly respond to current events or controversies. This real-time interaction gives you a significant edge over traditional media channels. You can respond instantly to controversies, rumors, or news that affects your campaign. Remember, your response should always align with your campaign's values and message.

With all the buzz around viral content, it might be tempting to aim for grand slams. However, the most successful social media strategies often rely on singles and doubles. Share valuable, reliable content and let the viral hits come naturally.

When it comes to promoting your content, it's not always about how much money you spend. Rather, it's about understanding how to use your resources wisely and effectively. Aim to boost posts that are resonating with your followers. Your aim should be to deepen engagement with these posts and extend their reach.

While organic reach is fantastic, don't underestimate the potential of targeted ads. Through these, you can easily reach segments of the audience who are likely to be interested in your campaign. Whether it's based on location, age, gender, or their likes, adjusting your Ad settings can maximize impact.

In addition, keep a close eye on your social media analytics. These provide useful insights into who your audience is, what they're interested in, and when they're online. Use these data to refine your strategy, content, and posting schedule. Remember, data analysis isn't just for your fundraising - it's for your outreach, too.

Collaboration is another key aspect of social media for campaigns. Look for opportunities to partner with influencers, community leaders, and even other politicians who share your values. These partnerships can broaden your reach and provide unique content opportunities.

Always remember, social media platforms are tools, not magic bullets. They are most effective when integrated with a comprehensive campaign strategy that combines digital with traditional methods of voter engagement, such as direct mail and door-to-door canvassing.

Lastly, while harnessing the power of social media, be mindful of digital ethics. Respect privacy, avoid negative or defamatory campaigns, and always be transparent with your followers about your intentions and your relationships with any partners or sponsors.

By developing a strategic approach, staying active and responsive, creating meaningful content, and maintaining transparency and respect for your followers, your campaign can leverage the powerful influence of social media in building voter support.

Of course, your social media campaign should align with your broader campaign narrative as one of a cohesive set of strategies to earn public confidence and, ultimately, win the competitive race. After all, elections aren't won online – they're won in the hearts and minds of voters. The online world is just one of the battlegrounds.

Chapter 8:
Mastering Public Speaking

The art of public speaking can very well act as the linchpin that tilts the playing field in your favor. It's not something you just 'have' or 'don't have'; it's a learnable craft. For a political career, your mastery over public speaking is not just about giving memorable speeches, it's also about handling media interviews with finesse. When crafting speeches, drill into a powerful and personal narrative that resonates with voters. Keep it succinct and filled with compelling soundbites for the media to latch onto. Remember, a powerful speech is a blend of the message, the delivery, and the timing. Now, for media interviews, preemptive preparation is key. Be ready for hard questions, and always answer with a candid demeanor. Finally, no matter how rehearsed or polished, your speech or response should feel spontaneous and from the heart. This combination of strategy, honesty, and passion is a surefire way to win over hearts and minds.

Crafting Impactful Speeches

As we move forward in our guide to launching a successful political career, it's time to focus on one of the most critical tools in your arsenal: the art of public speaking. Specifically, we'll delve into the craft of creating speeches that inspire, motivate, and win voters over to your side.

Engaging, eloquent, and captivating speeches can propel novice politicians into the national consciousness and elevate seasoned veterans to higher offices. Naturally, their significance in any political journey can't be overstated.

First, let's tackle the obvious question: What makes a speech impactful? The secret lies in a delightful blend of content and delivery. Your speech has to resonate with your audience, touch their sentiments, or, at the very least, make them think. It also needs to be delivered convincingly—it needs to weave a story, and you have to play the role of a compelling storyteller.

As you embark on creating your speech, start with something we'll call the 'Pillar Strategy.'. This strategy begins with figuring out three pillars, the key points you want your audience to walk away remembering. Keep these points concise and easy to understand; they will guide the rest of your speech and help keep it focused.

Remember to weave in your personal stories or experiences around these pillars. It not only humanizes you in front of the audience but also gives your speech a certain authenticity that is incredibly valuable. Stories create connection, spark emotion, and make it easier for the audience to remember your key points.

The best political stories are personal, relatable, and reinforce your campaign message. When constructing your narrative, aim to share experiences that resonate on a common, human level—not just as a politician, but as a member of your community. This shows voters that you understand their issues because you've lived them yourself.

It's also vital to anticipate your audience's reaction while writing your speech. Put yourself in their position and imagine how they may react to certain points or arguments. Try to provide answers to the questions they might have even before they've voiced them. Counter-arguments to possible dissent are also worth considering to maintain the flow of your narrative and fortify your position.

Beyond content, the emphasis you place on certain words and the rhythm of your speech also play a massive role in getting your message across. This is where your delivery comes into play. Practice varies your tone—know when to pause for dramatic effect and when to speak with more vigor to stress a point.

Body language also speaks volumes. Try to appear confident and authoritative throughout. Maintain steady eye contact as much as possible, use open and welcoming gestures, and avoid fidgeting or appearing too rigid. Remember, ultimately your body language should reinforce the impact and credibility of your words.

A quick pro-tip regarding the timeline of the speech: powerful openings and closings are essential. Average attention spans can be short, and you want the audience to be gripped from the beginning and to leave thinking about your final message. Give a powerful opening that gets people's attention and end with a rousing call-to-action to leave a lasting impression.

Speech-writing is an iterative process, and even the greatest orators in history didn't nail their speeches on the first try. Regular practice, fine-tuning, and a willingness to make adjustments based on feedback are critical. So, don't be afraid to rewrite, revise, and refine your speeches as you grow and improve your skills.

Finally, remember that truly impactful speeches not only motivate or inspire; they also reveal your authenticity as a politician. They convey your core beliefs, your commitment to serving your constituency, and the driving forces behind your campaign. This authenticity—this firm dedication to your mission—can sometimes be the deciding factor for voters on the fence.

As you embrace the art of crafting impactful speeches, remember that this is a chance to showcase who you are as a candidate, what you stand for, and how your leadership can positively impact your voters' lives. Engage your heart and your mind in the process, and the speeches you craft will resonate deeply with those who listen. These kinds of speeches have the power to inspire, persuade, and potentially win you that coveted office.

Handling Media Interviews

As you master your public speaking skills, a critical part of your training will involve mastering media interviews. They're inevitable in your political journey, regardless of your political level. These undoubtedly can be nerve-racking but they're also great opportunities to grant potential voters insight into your policy stances, your persona, and your leadership caliber.

First things first, understand the power of preparation for a media interview. Surprises are not your friend. The more information you have at your disposal, the better off you'll be. Start by knowing your interviewer's style, the show format, or the publication. Is it a hard-hitting daily news show or a laid-back local talk show? Identify what questions are likely to be fired at you and craft possible responses. A heads up, when strategizing answers, keep them concise, crisp, and sound bite friendly.

It's vital not to enter an interview defensively. Approach each question with a positive, constructive outlook. Take advantage of these moments to illustrate your capabilities, accomplishments, and goals. Also remember authenticity is key. Answer truthfully, because the voters value honesty above all else, and untruths can be spotted a mile away and can seriously hamper your credibility.

Moreover, non-verbal communication is as important as what you're saying. Make eye contact. Present a comfortable self. Dress appropriately. Maintain an encouraging body language. The audience and media will remember not just what you said, but also how you looked and presented yourself.

Develop an understanding of bridging techniques. Bridging is the act of tactfully directing the conversation to points you want to emphasize. By doing this, you can highlight your platform points regardless of the question asked. For instance, regardless of the question, you might say, "That's an interesting point, but what I believe is truly important is..." And then you can seamlessly transition to your desired topic.

You can't ignore how media operates. They love stories. So, when answering questions, where possible, narrate a story. These personal narratives can be incredibly effective at highlighting your political agenda, illustrating your passion, and most importantly, memorable to viewers and readers.

The way you interact with the press is equally important. Be respectful and professional, irrespective of the pressures of campaign life. Remember, they're the gateway to your audience. The media can lift you up or tear you down, depending on how you treat them. Building a healthy relationship with the press is pivotal.

Regulate any displays of emotion carefully. Certain situations may provoke frustration or anger. Be aware of this and manage it diligently because everything you do is visible. Present yourself as composed and levelheaded, even in the heat of the moment. People look for leaders who can handle pressure with grace.

During your interview, anticipate questions concerning your opposition. While it's tempting to launch into negativity, resist this urge. Name-calling and mudslinging will not endear you to voters. Focus on the facts, highlight policy differences, and maintain respect.

At the same time, one must not forget to be mindful of the questions that are out of bounds. Interviewers will sometimes ask personal or inappropriate questions. It's important to understand that it's okay to diplomatically refuse to answer certain questions if they're not related to your campaign or public service intentions.

Lastly, keep in mind that practice makes perfect. Regularly simulate interviews with your campaign team. Have them critique your responses, your body language, and overall delivery. Overcoming potential 'umms' and 'ahhs', refining your posture, and rehearsing your common talking points will boost your confidence in the real interview.

In conclusion, handling media interviews can initially seem daunting, but it's absolutely manageable with the right approach and adequate preparation. These interviews offer an unparalleled platform to deliver your messages and interact with the voters directly through the media. With the appropriate preparation and a positive attitude, you can transform media interviews into opportunities for engaging with the public and earning their trust.

And always remember, you're never just answering a question you're always showing the people who you are. Don't just use the interview as an opportunity to share your policies but use it to show your dedication, your personality, and most importantly, your commitment to serving the public.

Chapter 9:
Navigating Political Debates

After sharpening your public speaking skills in Chapter 8, it's time to apply those freshly honed talents to the fiercest battleground of all—political debates. Engagements of this sort are inevitable forums where your opponents and you will meet head-on to discuss and dispute policy, ideology, and leadership vision. To navigate these turbulent waters, you'll need to be well-prepared. Research your opponents, know their positions inside and out, and develop a deep understanding of how your policies contrast with theirs. Remember, debates are not just about proving you're right, but about emphasizing your opponent's inconsistencies and weaknesses, and highlighting the benefits of your positions. Additionally, you cannot overlook the importance of quick-thinking and sharp responses; therefore, be sure to practice real-time rebuttals. But don't get too embroiled in the war of words. Keep your cool and maintain a balance, demonstrating assertiveness blended with respect. In the next chapter, we'll help you navigate the final stages of your campaign as Election Day quickly approaches.

Preparing for Debates

Heading into a debate, like a seasoned marathon runner, requires a strategic mix of knowledge, preparedness, practice, and mental agility. The goal is not only to win the debate but to come across as professional, knowledgeable, and relatable. Let's roll up our sleeves and dive into understanding how to approach this critical aspect of your campaign.

Start with researching, which is the lifeline of any debate. Solid argumentation and compelling rebuttals are anchored in an in-depth understanding of the issues. Look into your opponent's history, their views, and statements on various matters, and be prepared for what they might bring up in the debate. You also need to have a firm grasp of your campaign policies, key messages, and the data or studies to support your points.

Secondly, know your debate format and understand the rules. Every debate – whether it's town hall style, a competing press conference, online or a traditional podium set up – comes with its own set of rules and format. Understanding the framework where the debate takes place can give you the upper hand by helping you refine your strategy and focusing on areas where you can make the most impact.

Thirdly, remember that a debate is not just about what you say, but how you say it too. The best content can be foiled by poor delivery. Practice your delivery, tone, pace, and body language until you can convey a message effectively under various conditions. Mock debates are incredibly useful as they mimic the pressure of the actual event. Don't shy away from recording your practice sessions, it will help you identify areas of improvement in your delivery and body language.

Being able to think on your feet is a much sought after skill in debates. Commonly known as extemporaneous speaking, the ability to make a persuasive argument without advanced preparation can make or break your performance. Practice this skill, perhaps by having team members throw unexpected questions at you during mock debates.

Additionally, remember to listen. Debating isn't just about getting your points across; it's also about responding to what your opponent is saying. Showing that you are actively listening not only helps adjust your strategy on the spot but also sends a powerful message to the audience that you care about other perspectives.

Handling negative attacks or criticisms from opponents gracefully is an imperative skill as well. Counterattacks may appear strong, but they can also come off as petty. The key is to stay poised, acknowledge the criticism if it's valid, and then reframe it in a way that supports your perspective or points out the flaw in your opponent's argument.

It's of utmost importance to remain consistent in your arguments. While you're agile on stage countering points and diplomatically handing criticisms, ensure your arguments are consistent with your campaign message. It might seem easy to get trapped in the heat of the moment and stray from your messaging - but remember, consistency is key.

Develop topic fluency. Not all topics will be in your comfort zone. Work on understanding a wide range of subjects. An expert presentation on a diverse set of topics can help voters trust your skills and judgment, even when the scenario is uncomfortable or unfamiliar.

An often overlooked aspect of preparing for debates is identifying a hook or a unique, compelling point that can be associated just with you. Having something distinctive can make you more memorable to voters and perhaps, tip the scales in your favor.

However, don't let all the strategy overshadow the authenticity. Voters can easily sense when a candidate is being sincere. While you prepare to the hilt, ensure your genuine self comes through. Show that you believe in your policies and that you're more than just a prepared candidate. Share examples, stories or anecdotes that reveal your personality or experiences can be particularly resonating.

Remember, the objective of the debate isn't solely winning an intellectual point scoring match. It is about connecting with the potential voters, demonstrating your capabilities, proving that you have the best ideas and plans, and having the right persona to represent them.

The monumental task of preparing for a political debate is all about striking a balance — between hard-hitting points and soft skills, between preparation and spontaneity, between strategy and authenticity. It's akin to walking a tightrope, but with time, practice, and a comprehensive understanding of the process, you'll find your footing. And when you do, you might discover that debating can be, not just a campaign necessity, but an exciting way to engage with the electorate.

Now that you understand how to prepare for debates, let's move on to another crucial aspect - how to actually win them. This involves finesse, strategic planning, and clever use of stagecraft. So let's sharpen the debating edge further in the next section: Strategies for Successful Debating.

Strategies for Successful Debating

Entering a political debate can feel like stepping into the gladiatorial arena. The heat of the lights, the anticipation in the air, and the knowledge that your every word and gesture will be scrutinized can be stressful. However, it's also an opportunity to showcase your policy knowledge, charisma, and the core values that make you a worthy candidate. Here are some strategies to help you thrive in this challenging environment.

Firstly, thoroughly understand your opponent's position. Familiarize yourself with their past legislative actions, public statements, and voting history. It's not enough to just know your position; you need to anticipate their responses and prepare rebuttals. Remember, political debate isn't only about declaring what you stand for, it's about engaging with your opponent's views and showcasing the benefits of your own.

Secondly, mind your own words. Always stick to consistent, clear messages. Repeating major points reinforces them in the minds of viewers and gives you a reputation for consistent thinking. However, be wary of coming off as a broken record; it's a fine line between reiteration and redundancy.

Next, remember that you're not just debating ideas with an opponent, you're connecting with an audience. Be empathetic and be conscientious of tone. Be approachable, authentic, and above all else, be respectful. Even when you disagree, and especially when you argue, it is critical that you respect your opponent. No one respects a bully.

Moreover, use simple, easy-to-understand language whenever possible. Your audience is as diverse as the nation itself. Losing them in complicated policy jargon won't win their hearts or their votes. Making complex ideas accessible is crucial.

Work on your body language and non-verbal cues as well. Effective debating isn't just about what you say, but how you say it. Body language, facial expressions, and tone of voice all contribute to your overall message. Gestures should be deliberate but not exaggerated. Eye contact is important, as it engages the viewer and projects confidence.

An absolute must-do before any debate is practice. Rehearse with your team, and simulate the debate conditions. Learn to deal with challenging questions under pressure. Use a timer to get used to the debate's rhythm and structure. Train yourself to deliver concise answers within the time limits.

Another significant element of strong debating is building your arguments. Construct and deconstruct points logically and clearly. This technique involves explaining your policy, demonstrating why that policy is needed, showing what it can do, and then opening up to potential rebuttals.

Always be on top of the facts and have data to support your points. A well-placed statistic or fact builds trust and credibility. However, be sure they are accurate and from reliable sources; your opponent won't hesitate to point out errors.

Be quick on your feet. Debates are independent events with their dynamics - a well-prepared message can get lost if you ignore what's happening in the moment. Gauge the reactions from the audience, the momentum of the debate, and react accordingly.

In the face of attacks, stay cool and composed. A good debater knows that criticism is inevitable. Instead of taking personal offense or lashing out, pivot the conversation back to your platform and ideas.

Meanwhile, when it comes to attacking your opponent, be strategic. Attack the policy, not the person. Personal attacks rarely win debates and could alienate voters who value civil discourse.

Lastly, use memorable closing statements. Debate statements are usually remembered by the first and last thing a speaker says. Use this cognitive bias to your advantage. Your closing statement should be compelling and sum up your argument effectively. Create an ending that refocuses the conversation back to your key ideas.

These strategies, while no guarantee of winning every debate, can strengthen your debating skills. With practice, patience, and the right approach, you can stride onto that stage with the knowledge that you're ready for whatever your opponent throws your way. Remember, an effective debater doesn't just argue. They persuade, they connect, they inspire.

So arm yourself with these strategies, and embrace the opportunity that debates bring - an opportunity to display your leadership, showcase your values, and communicate your vision for a future where your constituents are better represented and the nation moves forward.

Chapter 10:
The Home Stretch: Election Day

Now that you've mastered debates, delivered powerful speeches, and rallied significant voter support, it's time to cross the finish line as we hit Election Day. This chapter is all about the final campaign push and managing Election Day logistics, which is no small task. For your last campaign push, it's all hands on deck, and every minute counts. Make sure your team is reaching out to undecided voters, knocking on doors, and hitting the phones. Visits to polling booths could also tip the balance in your favor. It's all about maximizing visibility and contact. On the crucial day, ensure your 'Get out the Vote' (GOTV) operations are as efficient as they can be; this means having volunteers in place, assuring transportation for those who need it, and executing the polling place strategies you have planned. This day will likely be long, possibly stressful, but with effective planning and commitment, it can be fruitfully rewarding. So gear up, give it all you've got, because this is your moment to shine.

Final Campaign Push

The final days of a campaign can be the most exhilarating and nerve-racking part of the journey. It's a time when the months of exhaustive planning and campaigning culminate into what you hope will be a victorious conclusion. Whether you're the underdog or the frontrunner in the race, this section will provide advice for those last few vital moments. You're close to the finish line, so let's make this push count.

First off, it's essential to keep your campaign momentum going and intensify efforts where possible. The last stretch of the race needs to see a surge of your campaign presence, and it is no time for complacence. Reinforce your message to the public. Remember, there's still undecided voters out there who need just a little more convincing.

Your marketing and advertising strategies should be in top gear. Increase the frequency of your message on radio, TV or even through direct mails. If you've been saving up for a big ad push, now is the time to pull out the big guns. Only a few days are left for the voters to make up their minds and they should be continually seeing and hearing about you and your policies.

Don't forget about the power of social media. Share those last-minute campaign videos, post engaging content, and be ready to respond quickly to any hot topic that surfaces. Prepare a social media strategy that progressively escalates your campaign's visibility and presence as Election Day approaches.

Engage with your supporters in a meaningful way. Their energy can be instrumental in getting you over the finish line. Utilize your core supporters to encourage their networks via word of mouth, social media, or targeted canvassing. Ensure their efforts are aligned with your overall campaign message and theme.

In this final push, you might consider holding more public appearances and rallies. Make sure to target strategic locations where you can engage with substantial groups of supporters or undecided voters. Be available for voters to ask questions and discuss their concerns. This lends a personal touch and makes voters feel more invested in your campaign.

While addressing your audience, remember to remind them about the importance of their vote. It's essential for them to understand the value of their involvement and how crucial their role is in this democratic exercise. Never assume that your supporters are sold on your message. Repeat your core message and hammer the vision that you see for your constituency.

Media relationships at this point are equally crucial. Ensure your campaign's messaging and narrative remain consistent and positive in the media. This includes being available for last-minute interviews and willing to address any final concerns or allegations head-on.

The ground game will be vital in these final moments. Your door-to-door canvasing efforts should be robust and focused. You must remember to make personal connections with voters. People appreciate when a candidate takes time to talk to them, particularly at their doorstep.

An essential aspect of this ground operation is knowing your voters. They aren't just statistics on a page; they are human beings who want to feel heard and recognized. Make sure to keep your messaging personal and directly beneficial to them. Tailor your message to the audience's needs and wants—it will go a long way in making those coveted personal connections.

Lastly, express gratitude towards your campaign staff, volunteers, and supporters. Running for office is a collective effort and it's crucial to recognize everyone's contributions. Keep their morale high and make sure they know how much you appreciate their efforts.

No matter how well the campaign is going, be prepared for all possible outcomes. Whether the polls show you leading or lagging behind, don't let your guard down. Maintain your efforts, even if results start trending in your favor—elections can be unpredictable.

It's important to remember that even though the election season can be grueling, it is a privilege to run. Think about all that you've learned and the connections you've made. Cherish the journey. The road to Election Day is filled with challenges and victories, and the person you become in that process is someone to be proud of.

Try to enjoy these last few moments. It is an exhilarating time, filled with hard work, energy, action, and most of all, hope. Hope for a chance to make a difference, to serve the public, and to represent your constituency with integrity and dedication.

So, make the most of this final push. The home stretch of your campaign is not the time for slowing down—it's the time to give it your all. Good luck!

Election Day Logistics

Election day – the climax of your campaign journey is a whirl of events. It's like the Super Bowl for politicians. Brimming with anticipation, you might believe that your job is over once the votes start tumbling in, but it isn't. There are a load of logistics involved. Let's dive in.

Firstly, it's essential to have a comprehensive plan for Election Day. I mean it when I say that every little detail counts. The last thing you want is a hiccup out of the blue stunning your well-choreographed campaign. An efficient team can take the weight off your shoulders, disbursing responsibilities evenly, so the burden doesn't fall solely on you.

The day begins in the early morning hours. Your team should be ready to start their assignments before the polling stations open. It's vital to ensure that your poll watchers are prepared. Don't get dazzled by the term. Poll watchers are simply volunteers or staff who help monitor the polling stations for any irregularities that might affect the voting process or tallying of votes. They can be one of your greatest assets in maintaining a fair and square election.

Next comes one of the most critical parts of the election day logistics – voter transportation. You'd be surprised how many people want to vote but can't transport themselves to the polling stations. Managing voter transportation can be a pivotal part of your strategy. A coordinated effort can boost your vote count and shows voters that you truly care about their vote making a difference.

You've probably heard the phrase "get out the vote," or GOTV. Funny sounding, isn't it? But it's got nothing to do with a new TV show. It's an essential part of your Election Day campaign push. GOTV encompasses all those measures taken to encourage voters to go out and cast their votes. This could include efforts like telemarketing, mailing voting reminders, door-to-door canvassing, or even using digital platforms to encourage potential voters. Think creatively and pitch in everything you've got.

It's not just about asking people to vote. It's about making sure they can – smoothly and without obstacles. Take initiative to educate voters about their rights, remind them of their polling locations, guide them on the voting process, and yes - where required, offer any possible assistance.

Poll watching is another key activity for the day. It's not about spying on voters, of course. Still, it involves having volunteers oversee the process at polling places to ensure that everything is going according to plan. They're there to observe, report inconsistencies, or assist voters if they notice errors. It's one of the ways you can proactively prevent voter suppression and ensure a fair election.

While managing these disparate parts, don't forget to take care of your staff. They've been on this journey with you, spending unbearable amounts of coffee-fueled nights working their socks off. Ensure they have the necessary relief, food, supplies, and transportation. Remember, their well-being and morale can significantly impact overall productivity and performance on this critical day.

Things are bound to get intense as the day progresses, and it's easy for tempidity to take hold. Communication then becomes vital. Regular check-ins throughout the day will keep the team oiled and working in sync. Establish a central contact or use group messaging apps to keep everyone on the same page. Think of it as your campaign's batphone – every member should know the number to call for immediate assistance or to report issues.

When the polls close, make sure you have a plan in place for collecting and keeping an eye on results. The digital age has made things easier with real-time election result tracking. However, it never hurts to have a backup method for collecting data, especially in case of sudden technical issues.

The end of election day doesn't mean it's time to breathe a sigh of relief. Now comes verification and sometimes contestation. It's your poll watchers' responsibility to ensure the vote count matches the records and report any inconsistencies. The integrity of this process is crucial and serves to confirm the accuracy of the election results.

Election Night, a.k.a. The Long Night, is more about waiting and watching. While it might seem like all you can do is chew your nails and nervously watch the hours slip by, it's actually a great opportunity to go live on social media platforms to thank your supporters and keep your campaign's spirit high during these crucial moments.

So there you have it; Election Day is more than just waiting for votes to roll in. It requires a meticulous combination of management, communication, and multitasking. With a solid plan, the right team, and a strong cup of coffee, you're ready to take on Election Day and every challenge it throws at you. Remember, it's not just about winning - but also how you play the game.

Chapter 11:
Post-Election Analysis

Now that the election's dust has settled, it's time for some in-depth analysis, irregardless of whether you've won or lost. It's crucial to conduct an honest evaluation of your campaign in order to understand what worked, what didn't, and where improvements can be made. Start by unraveling your campaign's narrative and voter feedback, while closely studying the voting data. Pore over the geographical areas where you gleaned significant support, as well as those regions where you fell short. Understand the demographics of your supporters, and where your opponent outpaced you. It's not about delineating fault, but extracting lessons to better equip you for future campaigns or, if you're victorious, governing effectively. Don't forget to acknowledge your team's hard work and keep the passion burning. Through it all, remember this: a single election doesn't define your political journey. Make your analysis about growth, improvement, and a relentless pursuit of public service. Keep your eyes on the target, and always plan for the next big step.

Learning from Election Results

Your experience in the electoral race, whether victorious or not, offers a goldmine of lessons. One of the key tasks after an election is to analyze and learn from the results. Let's dive into how we can do this effectively.

First and foremost, you need to understand the numbers. What was your votes percentage? How did you perform in different demographics, locations, and social groups? Look at the data from every angle you can – this info isn't just a snapshot of the recent past, it's a roadmap to potential futures.

If you've won, congratulations! Celebrate, but remember that in political life, your next campaign begins the day after the victory. There's always another election around the corner. Therefore, use this opportunity to understand what worked for you. What were the key elements that helped secure the majority's favor? Was it your positioning on specific issues, your public speaking skills, or your ability in relation to your competitor?

On the flip side, if you've lost, don't be too hard on yourself. Defeat, while bitter, is an opportunity to learn, grow, and come back stronger. It might be tempting to forget the whole thing and move on, but taking the time to understand where and how things didn't go as planned will be immensely beneficial for your future endeavors.

Did you miss the mark with certain voting blocs? Were there any contentious issues that you failed to address convincingly? Was your campaign visibility not as high as your opponents'? Ask these tough questions and work with your team to find the answers.

Remember, no effort is wasted in a campaign. Even initiatives that didn't yield expected results teach valuable lessons about what might work next time. It's not about framing things as 'failure', but as an investment in your political learning curve. So, take that 'failed' grassroots campaign or that less-than-inspiring speech and ask yourself what you can draw from them.

Beyond your own performance, you should also scrutinize your rivals'. There's much you can learn from their campaigns - successful or otherwise. How had they differentiated themselves? What issues did they focus on? How involved were they in the local community? What strategies did they use to capture voter attention and trust?

Comparing your campaign strategies and their resulting outcomes with those of your competitors can illuminate new approaches and offer insights for your own political journey. But remember, it's not about imitating others. It's about learning and adapting strategies to suit your style and principles.

Post-election analysis isn't just about the candidate. It is also about the team. Gather your campaign team and discuss the highs and lows. What were their observations? What insights do they have about the campaign, the voters, the issues, the logistics? Their perspectives can offer remarkably fresh insights.

Learning from election results is a process that requires humility, honesty, and a strong resolve. It can be arduous to revisit a tough campaign trail, but remember, in politics, as in life, the best lessons are often learned in the hardest times. Like they say, what doesn't kill you makes you stronger.

Lastly, don't forget to look at the broader picture. Every election, whether local, state, or federal, influences and is influenced by the national political climate. It's important to understand how your election fits into that broader narrative. How are politics shifting locally, regionally, and nationally? How can you adapt to these trends in your future campaigns?

This broader reflection helps you to stay relevant in a constantly changing political landscape. It offers you a chance to reaffirm your political beliefs, challenge old ideas, and incorporate new ones.

Remember, the goal here is not just to win an election, but to become an effective and well-loved public servant. And for that, learning from every experience, including election results, is paramount. So, embrace the journey, absorb the lessons, and prepare for the next challenge. After all, politics isn't a sprint. It's a marathon.

Planning for the Future

Now that the election has ended, and you've analyzed the outcome, it's time to start planning for the future. Regardless of whether you won or lost, the political journey doesn't stop here. In fact, it's just beginning. So, let's discuss how best to prepare for what's next on your political path.

Start your journey with an assessment, using your post-election analysis as a guide. If you've emerged victorious in the election, examine what worked in your favor. Could it have been your campaign strategy? Was it your effective communication skills? Or perhaps your political platform resonated strongly with voters. Determining the catalysts for your victory is crucial in preparing for the future. It helps you understand what to keep doing or replicating in future campaigns or, for incumbents, to maintain during their term.

On the other hand, if you've lost, it's crucial, but daunting, to assess what went wrong. However, keep your chin up because losing an election isn't the end of your political career. Plenty of successful politicians lost their first few elections. Use your loss as a stepping stone to future success. Learn from your mistakes and start preparing to come back stronger.

Undeniably, your future planning should involve crafting an effective strategy for maintaining or building voter support. This might mean continuing with the same voter outreach strategies if they worked or revising them if they didn't. Aim to establish an ongoing relationship with your voters. Stay connected, remain visible, attend local events, and maintain an active social media presence. The objective should always be to remain relevant to your constituents, even outside of the campaign period.

Beyond elections, consider the legislative goals you want to achieve in your term for those who won or are incumbents. Your political career isn't only about winning elections. It's about making a difference and impacting change. It might help to revisit your political platform and pinpoint key issues that you want to address. As you work towards these goals, know that they will have an impact on your eligibility and success in future elections.

Consider shedding light on your work and achievements. Transparency is key in maintaining public trust. Regularly update your constituents on your progress, hurdles overcome, and the results of your initiatives. This practice not only involves your supporters in your journey but also builds a strong case for your re-election.

For those who find themselves on the losing side, all is not lost. Use your post-election period to rebuild and strategize. Evaluate your candidacy, your campaign message, and your outreach strategies. Each of these elements can influence your chances of success in your next campaign. Don't be afraid to pivot or overhaul if you discover inefficiencies.

Another step is to continually develop your skills. Excellent public speaking, negotiation, leadership, and networking skills are timelessly valuable. No matter where you are in your political journey, these skills will always play a crucial role. Take your downtime as an opportunity to refine your skills. Engage in professional development courses, attend seminars, or seek a mentor in your political field.

Remember to nurture your networks as well. The relationships you built during your campaign with donors, volunteers, and voters shouldn't end there. Keep your relationships active and mutually beneficial. You never know who could help elevate your career. Networking is not a one-time effort, but a continuous process.

Maintaining financial readiness is another important aspect of future planning. Irrespective of your election outcome, the funds need to keep flowing. As the saying goes, "money is the sinew of war," which also applies to politics. Keep in touch with your donors to ensure the financial robustness of your future campaigns.

While strategizing what lies ahead, consider adopting a broad perspective. Allow room for unexpected opportunities and challenges. The political landscape is ever-evolving. Be open to expanding your portfolio and stepping into a variety of roles. This adaptability will provide you with a holistic political experience, set you apart from your competitors, and provide added agility.

Lastly, always revisit and reassess your political goals. Your ambitions should guide your future planning. Whether it's to run for a higher office, implement a revolutionary policy, or build a stronger party foundation, your goals should reflect in your strategy and shape your political future. Remember, your ability to achieve these goals lies in your resilience, your readiness to adapt, and your dedication to serve the people.

As you move forward in your political journey, remember that election outcomes are just one aspect of a deeper, lifelong commitment to service. Embrace the journey, learn from your experiences, stay dedicated, and continue to strive for the best, because the future of political success belongs to those who believe in the beauty of their dreams and work diligently to achieve them.

Chapter 12:
Extra Tips to Triumph in U.S. Elections

In the previous chapters, we've laid out the foundation you'll need to plan and conduct a successful political campaign. Now, we'll discuss unconventional tips and hacks that can give you the edge in these competitive arenas. So, let's dive right in.

Interception - Know Your Opponent's Game

You can't win in politics without understanding your opponent's strategy. It's not enough to just highlight why you're the best choice - you'll also need to identify the weaknesses in your opponents' campaign and find effective ways to exploit them. However, it's vital to keep this in check - mudslinging is never an effective long-term strategy and can backfire, damaging your reputation.

Relevance to Current Events

A tip that often swings the pendulum in favor of the savvy candidate is staying up-to-date with current events and being able to weave these into campaign rhetoric. By relating your policies and stances to real-world events, you can drive home the relevancy of your campaign and show voters that you're in touch with what's happening on the ground.

Optimize on Policy

No matter how charismatic a candidate, the backbone of any strong campaign is well-crafted policy. Speak to a wide range of constituents, from industry professionals to everyday workers. This insight into the needs and perspectives of your voters will allow you to create policies that resonate with a large portion of the electorate.

Create a Compelling Narrative

Storytelling is a powerful tool in politics. Crafting a compelling narrative about yourself and your intentions helps voters relate to you. Be honest, be vulnerable, and let people see what has driven you to serve. It's this personal connection that can often bridge the divide in tight races.

Don't Neglect Traditional Media

While social media campaigns are crucial in the modern age, don't overlook the power of traditional media outlets. Newspapers, radio, and local TV stations can still heavily influence public opinion. Be sure to press the flesh, establish good relationships with media personnel, and take every opportunity to utilize these outlets.

Consistency is Key

Nothing harms a campaign more than a candidate who flip-flops on issues. Be clear about your beliefs and maintain a consistent message throughout your campaign. Even if you do refine your stance over time, ensure that it's communicated as an evolution rather than an about-face.

Synergy Between Online and Offline Campaigns

Make sure there's synergy between your online and offline efforts. The messages you convey through social media must resonate with what you're saying offline, in speeches and debates. This consistency creates a cohesive and powerful campaign that penetrates deeply into the psyche of the voter.

Mobilize the Youth

Young people are a potent force in politics, often generating infectious enthusiasm that can invigorate your campaign. So, pay special attention to policies that matter to younger voters – education, technology, the environment – and make sure they are represented within your team. Their passion can just be the spark you need.

Be Ready for the Long Haul

Political campaigns aren't sprints; they're marathons. Prepare yourself, your team, and your family for the long haul. Stamina, patience, and resilience are the fuels that power the long journey to the polling booth.

Trust Your Instincts

Lastly, be sure to trust your instincts. As a candidate, you are the embodiment of your campaign and ultimately, the decisions you make will shape success. Listen to advice, take guidance, but at the end of the day trust in your ability to lead.

Success in the political arena doesn't come easy. It's an intricate game of strategy, charisma, and grit. But by using the tips outlined in this chapter, you can position yourself to not just participate, but to triumph in U.S. elections.

Conclusion

As we come to the end of our journey exploring the intricacies of running for office in America, it's clear just how rich and intricate the political landscape can be. It is a path that requires preparation, dedication, resilience, and a genuine passion for service. You've walked through understanding the political system, choosing the right office, building your core team, and masterfully navigating through election day and beyond.

Dedication to understanding the U.S. political system is your foundation. The complex network of Federal, State, and local elections, and the distinct roles within each, offers a broad range of opportunities to serve and effect change. Services and power are distributed across different offices, and a thorough understanding is essential. This foundation underpins your political career decisions, platform development, and all other aspects of your campaign.

Recognizing your strengths, values, and passions is the first step in choosing the right office. Understanding where you can make a difference encourages you to be proactive, fostering a sense of purpose and creating opportunities for service. Similarly, the people you choose to include in your core team are another key component in your journey. These individuals should supplement your skills, offering expertise in areas such as campaign management, policy advising, and media relations.

Your political platform is both your compass and your bridge to voters. It should reflect your understanding of mainstream issues, and the needs and aspirations of the masses you aim to serve. This platform, coupled with well-rounded campaign fundraising strategies and stringent adherence to campaign finance laws, keeps your campaign on track and viable.

Connecting with voters lies at the heart of any successful political career. Through effective outreach strategies, grassroots mobilization, and the strategic use of social media, you can build a support base that not only votes for you, but champions your cause. This connection provides the energy and driving force behind the campaign.

Public speaking and debate skills complement your ability to connect with voters. They enable you to articulate your platform, handle media interviews effectively, and take on political debates with confidence. These skills ensure that your message resonates, that it reaches far and wide, and that it inspires confidence and loyalty among voters.

The home stretch leading up to Election Day is a call for reevaluation, intensity, and focus. Your ground game must be strong, your message clear, and your campaign logistics flawlessly executed. This culmination is the moment to galvanize your supporters and display the full force of your campaign's momentum.

Regardless of the election outcome, there is always room for growth and learning. Post-election analysis helps you understand where you've succeeded, and where you can do better. Planning for the future, equipped with this knowledge, ensures you continue to build on your strengths and address areas of improvement.

Finally, remember, the road to success in U.S. politics is not for the faint of heart. It takes grit, perseverance, and an unwavering commitment to serve. It involves taking risks, moving outside your comfort zone, and continually striving to connect with voters. It often includes facing intense scrutiny, navigating complex regulations, and working exhaustively.

However, it's also a road filled with the ability to enact real, tangible change. Being a part of the democratic process means being a part of something bigger than yourself. It offers the opportunity to influence policy and effect change that could improve the lives of many. It's a rewarding and noble pursuit, commanding respect and admiration from all corners of society.

The journey ahead could be tough, fulfilling, and incredibly rewarding, all at once. Be persistent. Stay focused. Be true to your values and continue to strive for excellence in all aspects of your campaign. Running for office isn't just about winning an election, it's about embodying the change you wish to see and inspiring others with your vision.

In conclusion, with the right approach, including strategic planning, strong team building, effective campaign strategies, and a dedicated spirit, you can join the rank of those who have run for office, and won. Stay true to your intentions, connect authentically with voters, and never forget why you embarked on this journey. This will not only help you win an election but also solidify your legacy in the annals of American politics.

Here's to future leaders, change-makers, and dedicated public servants. Your commitment to filling such incredible roles contributes significantly to continually reshaping the vibrant narrative that is America. May this guide serve you well on your journey. Good luck, and may your name be etched positively in the chronicles of American history.

Appendix A:
Useful Resources for
Aspiring Politicians

So, you're ready to dive into the world of politics, you've absorbed these chapters, and you're primed with knowledge and insight to launch your political career. However, the journey is just beginning, and you'll need more resources to help you navigate the political landscape. This appendix contains a list of comprehensive resources that you can refer to as you embark on this journey.

Understanding the Political System

The U.S. Constitution: Get your hands on a copy of this document and familiarize yourself with the laws of the land. It's available online at *www.constitutionus.com*.

The Federalist Papers: It's a collection of essays written by Alexander Hamilton, James Madison, and John Jay promoting the ratification of the United States Constitution. Understanding these can give a deeper insight into the intentions of the founding fathers. They're available online for free at *www.thefederalistpapers.org*.

C-SPAN.org: It's a great resource to learn about the inner workings of the government. It provides gavel-to-gavel coverage of U.S. House and Senate floor proceedings.

Books to Understand Politics and Elections

"Running for Office: The Strategies, Techniques and Messages Modern Political Candidates Need to Win Elections": This book by Ronald A. Faucheux provides a bird's eye view of the world of politics.

"The Art of Political Campaigning": It's written by Frank Bush, a seasoned political consultant. It provides practical advice on running successful campaigns.

"Hardball: How Politics Is Played, Told by One Who Knows the Game": Written by Chris Matthews, it's a book that explores the practical aspects of politics.

Training Programs & Classes

There are many institutions and organizations that offer classes, workshops, and courses specially designed for aspiring politicians:

American University Campaign Management Institute: This organization offers intensive training seminars on different aspects of campaign management.

The Leadership Institute: They offer workshops, training programs, and resources on various aspects of politics from public speaking to campaign strategy.

Software and Tech Tools

Modern political campaigns are heavily reliant on technology:

Voter Gravity (www.votergravity.com): This is an advanced campaign and voter contact platform that helps you manage and streamline campaigns.

ActBlue (www.actblue.com): ActBlue is a nonprofit technology organization that enables Democrats, progressive groups, and nonprofits to raise money online.

Networking and Professional Organizations

Networking is an integral part of politics, and joining these organizations can provide valuable exposure and contacts:

Young Democrats of America (www.yda.org): An organization that champions young Democrats and helps them get involved in the political process.

National Federation of Republican Women (www.nfrw.org): An organization that aims to foster women's leadership within the Republican Party.

These resources will serve as a valuable companion, bolstering the knowledge and strategies outlined in this book. But remember, there's no replacement for direct experience. Meet people, seek out mentors, immerse yourself in the community, and start forging your political path.

Glossary

Below, you'll find a list of key terms, phrases and terminologies that you may come across while reading this guide. The aim is to provide convenient definitions that will help ensure a smooth, enlightening reading process.

Campaign Manager: This is the individual charged with leading the campaign team. They're responsible for planning and executing a successful political campaign.

Campaign Fundraising: This refers to the systematic collection of campaign funds, usually in the form of donations or contributions, to promote a political candidate or idea.

Election Day: This is the day when registered voters across a jurisdiction cast their ballots for their preferred candidates or choices on various issues.

Federal Elections: These are elections held at the national level to choose federal office holders such as the President, Senators, and Representatives.

Grassroots Mobilization: This is a political campaign or movement strategy where ordinary citizens are urged to participate, usually in tasks like volunteering, spreading the campaign message, or voting.

House of Representatives Elections: These are Federal Elections that occur every two years across all 435 districts in the United States, to elect representatives to the lower house, or the House of Representatives.

Political Career Direction: This refers to the course or path that a person decides to take in their political journey, often determined by their ambitions, strengths, experiences, and the offices they seek to hold.

Political Debates: These are organized discussions, usually in a public forum, where political candidates express their views on pertinent issues to inform and influence voters.

Political Platform: This refers to the set of values, objectives, and policy proposals a candidate promotes as part of his or her campaign, with an aim of winning voter support.

Presidential Election: This is a national election that takes place every four years to elect the president and vice president of the United States.

Senate Elections: These are Federal Elections occurring every two years, where a third of the United States Senate seats are up for grabs.

Social Media: This refers to digital tools and platforms that enable users to create, share, and exchange information, predominantly online, a potential game-changer in political campaigns.

State Elections: These are elections, often concurrent with Federal Elections, where voters select office-holders for state governance, like Governors or state representatives.

Voter Outreach Strategies: These are planned and focused efforts made by a campaign to engage, inform, and interact with potential and registered voters. It often includes canvassing, phone banking, and digital outreach efforts.

This collection of terminology isn't exhaustive, but it should equip you with enough background to understand some core elements of running for office in the United States. As you delve deeper into the world of U.S. politics, you'll naturally come across new terms, laws, and concepts—but don't fret! Embrace each as an opportunity to grow and gain a deeper understanding of this compelling field.

www.ingramcontent.com/pod-product-compliance
Lightning Source LLC
Chambersburg PA
CBHW030403290526
45785CB00004B/1884